KT-238-800

Leisurely Gardening

Other gardening books published by Christopher Helm

NIGEL COLBORN

Leisurely Gardening

A Laissez-Faire Guide to the Low-Maintenance Garden

CHRISTOPHER HELM

London

© 1989 Nigel Colborn
Line illustrations by David Henderson
Text designed by Malcolm Harvey Young
Christopher Helm (Publishers) Ltd, Imperial House,
21–25 North Street, Bromley, Kent BR1 1SD

ISBN 0-7470-0421-8

A CIP catalogue record for this book is available from
the British Library

All rights reserved. No reproduction, copy or
transmission of this publication may be made
without written permission.

No paragraph of this publication may be reproduced,
copied or transmitted save with written permission or
in accordance with the provisions of the Copyright
Act 1956 (as amended), or under the terms of any
licence permitting limited copying issued by the
Copyright Licensing Agency, 7 Ridgmount Street,
London WC1E 7AE.

Any person who does any unauthorised act in relation
to this publication may be liable to criminal
prosecution and civil claims for damages.

Typeset by Paston Press, Loddon, Norfolk
Printed and bound in Great Britain by Hollen Street Press Ltd, Berkshire

CONTENTS

To my parents, Leslie and Anne Colborn, whose upbringing was far from *laissez-faire*, thank goodness, but who led me to discover the joy of the garden.

COLOUR PLATES

1. Bold planting of perennials in mixed borders.
2. A boldly planted edge, chives used here, can 'bind' loose planting together.
3. A terrace planted with sage, *Osteospermum* 'Weetwood' and helianthemums.
4. One of the author's gravel gardens.
5. A well developed shrubby border with varying foliage highlighted by the golden hop *Humulus* 'Aurea'.
6. Laced pink 'Valerie Finnis' with dark foliaged sedum 'Bertram Anderson' on pea gravel.
7. A seedling helianthemum which arrived in the author's gravel.
8. Wall plants, like these *Erinus* will seed themselves naturally once established.
9. A fine *Papaver somniferum*. Selected by weeding out inferior colours.
10. A colony of *laissez-faire* annuals: Cornflowers, *Salvia horminum* and *Glaucium phoenicium*.
11. Wall top furnished with *Cheiranthus* 'Moonlight'.
12. A red-leaved form of wild woodspurge, *Euphorbia amygdaloides* 'Rubra' growing with the Turkish native *Omphalodes cappadocica*.
13. Ox-eye daisies (*Chrysanthemum leucanthemum*) and red campion (*Silene dioica*) used as cottage garden plants.
14. Red admiral (*Vanessa atalanta*) on *Aster novi-angliae*.
15. Stepping stones make walking on grit more pleasant.
16. *Laissez-faire* planting but a strict colour scheme—blue and yellow.
17. Tree paeonies and columbines—a happy association.
18. Snowdrops and *Cyclamen coum* begin the year's display.
19. Colchicums used here as foliage plants. The leaves can become untidy.
20. *Fritillaria meleagris*. The white form of snake's head.
21. *Clematis* 'H.F. Young', a reliable early bloomer with *Cirsium rivulare* 'Atro-purpureum' in front.
22. The cyclamineus hybrids are good for naturalising: 'Peeping Tom' and 'February Gold'.
23. The rugosa hybrid 'Mrs Anthony Waterer'. Superb scent, good disease resistance.
24. *Papaver orientale* 'Goliath'. The reddest of all big poppies.

FIGURES

ACKNOWLEDGEMENTS

My grateful thanks to all fellow gardeners who, by their good counsel, have helped me to crystallise my own ideas on gardening for today. Especial salutations to John Codrington, whose Rutland garden is a fine example of *laissez-faire*; to Beth Chatto, who knows exactly how to put interesting plants to good use and to Lady Anne Palmer, who frequently reminds me – obsessed as I am with herbaceous subjects – of the great diversity of woody plants which lend themselves to modern gardening.

Particular thanks to my children, for putting up with a grumpy and pre-occupied father during the preparation of this book (and at other times) and to my wife, Rosamund, for reading my halting prose and for helping me to carefully avoid splitting infinitives and dangling phrases.

Finally, the Royal Horticultural Society. We often take their superb facilities such as the Lindley Library, Wisley and the Vincent Square shows for granted, but I have learnt much from belonging to the Society and the gratitude I express here is deeply felt.

N.C.
1989

CHAPTER ONE

Basic Principles

We gardeners are in manacles. Oppressed by the tyranny of the past, we try, valiantly, to maintain standards set in an age when labour was cheap and time plentiful. Or, far worse, we give in to the pressure of modern life and opt for a set of dreary compromises with nature, involving ground covers, clumps of shrubs, instant displays and frightening areas of fake stone and concrete called 'patios' or 'yards', depending on where we live.

The object of this book is to show you how modern gardening, in spite of limited time, limited space and the likelihood of your moving house within the next few years, can be as rewarding an art form as in the golden Edwardian years. In those days, trend-setters like Gertrude Jekyll and William Robinson were laying the foundations for a kind of gardening that still persists today, even though it doesn't suit us or our lifestyle at all. Harking back to the good old days, when most middle-class people could afford a gardener, is great fun. Everyone enjoys an occasional wallow in nostalgia, but we should interpret historical methods with great care.

Picture, say, a typical plot in one of London's *nicer* suburbs in the early 1920s. It might have run to more than an acre. Immaculate lawns would have been hemmed in by enormous herbaceous borders where all the plants were individually staked and tied. There would have been a rose garden with a hundred or so hybrid teas, every one pruned in March, fed with dung, sprayed monthly and deadheaded throughout the season. In the front, perhaps a formal area with shaped beds in the lawn. These would have been planted out twice a year – tulips and forgetmenots or wallflowers for spring; salvias, petunias or African marigolds for summer. There would have been a little orchard with apples, plums and pears; a kitchen garden growing potatoes, green vegetables, soft fruit and flowers for cutting. In short, enough to keep a man in work for forty or fifty hours a week.

Today, though the manicured part of my own garden stretches to about 2½ acres (1 ha) I am able to maintain it to a reasonable standard doing little more than weekend work. True, I have help – a chap mows the lawns once a week – but we have a rose garden, rock gardens, mixed borders, shrubberies and a collection of more than 3,000 different plant species and hybrids. We open to the public regularly during the spring and summer – usually winning the praises of the horticultural *cognoscenti* who visit.

So it is possible, and desirable, to garden well without labour and with limited time.

More important, it is possible to *enjoy* every aspect of the garden without opting out and going for concrete, without carpeting every available space with evergreen ground cover and without breaking your back.

The *laissez-faire* approach

Gardening without effort requires a knack – a secret ingredient. The basis for success is *laissez-faire* – I'm sorry there's no comfortable English equivalent – meaning literally, 'let act' (Oxford Dictionary) or more loosely, 'let it do its own thing'. The gist is to make the garden itself do as much of the work as possible. Leave as much to nature as you possibly can. 'Oh sure!' you might say. 'Abandon the whole thing and let anarchy happen.' But you'd be wrong. You *do* control the inputs and you must keep a check on certain pressure points – all to be covered in detail later – but by and large, your attitude in the garden becomes more liberal. Freedom in the garden, as in society, must be tempered with responsibility.

What do we want *from our garden?*

We want recreation, relaxation and enjoyment. The garden is:

Somewhere for the children to play
Somewhere to build up our plant collection
A wildlife refuge
A venue for outdoor parties
A place to meditate
A means of impressing visitors
A source of exercise
A food source
Somewhere to hide
A place to sit and read

– in short, a universal amenity.

What do we not want *from our garden?*

We do not want hassle. The garden must not be:

A millstone
A worry
A never ending chore
Somewhere to develop back ache
An eyesore
A source of shame
A hated space
A haven for pests

Above all, we do not want it to be *boring*.

Making a choice

All this boils down to what you perceive as your ideal garden. Would you prefer it to offer more, but to take less looking after? Since you are bothering to read a book about it, and have got this far, it is probably safe to assume that you are reasonably keen. However, unlike your Edwardian ancestors who merely pointed an authoritative finger at the weeds and told the staff to see to them, you are being pulled in several different directions by urgent demands on your time. Both partners may have full-time employment – an Edwardian lady never worked. Middle-class children were packed off to boarding school at tender ages and not seen for three months at a time. Nowadays, parents are expected to be at school nearly as frequently as their offspring and so on and so on. Time is money and time is short!

To many people, lounging round a swimming pool or burning meat on a charcoal grill amounts to the ultimate Sunday satisfaction. And why not? But even with your sights set as low as that, wouldn't the pool and barbecue areas be more pleasant if they were carefully planted to provide interest all the time without adding to the maintenance work? If you want to stretch out on a comfortable lounger, what would you rather smell? Chlorine from the pool? Or would you prefer the aroma of the sizzling steaks to be enhanced by scent from rosemary, wild thyme, sage and clove pinks growing over the flagstones all around you? In winter – which lasts in England from September to May – do you want to look out onto a garden where January blossoms twinkle like jewels on a grey worsted outfit or will the sight of the half-empty pool and dead geraniums in the plastic Georgian urns satisfy your aesthetic cravings for the season? Assuming the extra work is minimal, the choice should be reasonably easy to make!

Having made our choice, we shall have to therefore exercise some discipline in putting it to work.

Discipline

A nasty word for us liberal (please note the small 'l') gardeners, but a little self-discipline will enable you to save so much time. Successful *laissez-faire* gardening depends on discipline even though that may sound like self-contradiction. The secret is to *keep abreast*. Most heavy gardening jobs become necessary because things have been left too long. Weeds must not be allowed to seed. If they do, the problems are compounded. A hasty whip through a weedy area, pulling the worst and concentrating on anything about to go to seed is far better than a thorough fork through if you are pressed for time and unlikely to finish. This goes against the good old Victorian ethic of doing the job well or not at all. But does it? If the most effective cure for weeds is to prevent them from reproducing, perhaps it is better to do that, even if the border still looks a bit messy where you've been, than to begin a painstaking overhaul, failing to finish before it's too late.

As one of the world's slobs, I hesitate to preach about tidiness. My own tool shed falls a long way short of ideal but I do try to start each season with everything in its place. Spending hours searching for missing items is bound to build up *angst* and can soon ruin a good gardening day.

Managing your time efficiently has little to do with gardening, but setting aside a minimum number of hours per month is no bad thing. Better still is to decide on a certain amount of work per week and sticking to that. Wet/dry alternatives, especially in the English climate are helpful, but not always possible. Where the sun shines more reliably, planning is easier. Even ten minutes a day can achieve an amazing amount. This is particularly so where routine maintenance is concerned. In my garden, a great deal of the area is weeded by hand. Even if I'm waiting, say, for someone to open the door, I pull up a handful or so. A host of other specific labour- and time-saving strategies will emerge as we go through the book. At this stage, however, it pays to look at the whole concept. We must always weigh the cost in time against the results. Avoid plants which need a lot of attention unless they are likely to reward you with a fantastic show or unless you happen to have a penchant for them. Hedges are a splendid garden feature, for example, but it pays to grow only those that need a single annual clip. Thus, privet, *Lonicera nitida* and hawthorn are out. But yew, beech, hornbeam and holly give plenty of scope for formal hedging and a great wealth of flowering shrubs make charming informal hedges needing scant attention.

How to go about it

Some of the work described in the following chapters will appear to be heavy and difficult. This is because part of the text describes how to set up your *laissez-faire* garden from scratch or how to convert existing structures to new uses. Rather than having a single chapter on major constructions, it seems more appropriate to include them where they are most relevant. Don't be put off by the scale of some of the jobs. They are always far worse on paper than in reality – I've carried out most of them single-handed in my garden and the labour and time they have saved are immeasurable.

Wonderful though it may be, to be able to make use of the best available raw materials, cost is always a frightening element. As well as diverse demands on our time, many of us have pressing demands on our purses as well. I have used the cheapest available materials in my illustrations because those are what I have used in my own garden. Sometimes it shows. How I'd love to replace, for instance, my concrete flags with real York stone and throw my rustic seats onto a huge bonfire. A collection of beautifully designed iroko hardwood garden furniture could take their places but, at their price it isn't very likely!

With plants, I have never tried to economise. There is no need because, in relation to anything else in a garden they are so cheap. Propagation is often simplicity itself, particularly with non-woody plants. (Anything that isn't a tree, shrub or a woody climber is non-woody.) If your plant budget is kept strictly for those items that are difficult to propagate and, at the same time, you increase your circle of horticultural acquaintances, the source of new plant material available to you will be almost unlimited. Most clubs and societies have seed exchange schemes and, even if at first the flow of seeds between the society and you seems to be largely one way, there will be a future in which you could figure as a valuable source to others. Gardening is a cooperative hobby. Gardeners worth their salt love to share their material as well as their triumphs and disasters.

So now that you have a rough idea of what the *laissez-faire* approach to gardening is about, you should be ready to move on to some specifics.

Getting started

Not all gardening activities are universally pleasant and interesting. So, what puts people off gardening? Hard work? Compulsion? Let's have a look, first, at the most irksome jobs. They are, in diminishing order of unpleasantness:

Digging All the textbooks of the last hundred years go to great lengths on digging. There are hundreds of instructions and techniques – all tending to nip any beginner's enthusiasm in the bud. Perhaps the concepts sprang from the Victorian philosophy which says: 'It's only doing you any good if it hurts.' A classic reason for deep tilling was that it enabled one to open up the soil and dig in muck. But the facts, as far as soil biology is concerned, suggest that heavy digging is a complete waste of time. Humus can be worked into the soil in other ways and deep down below the surface, organic matter is unnecessary. High levels of compost or rotting vegetation in the soil actually *increase* the need for nitrogen – but more of that later. As far as your health is concerned, you won't have turned many sods before you find out that digging is extremely bad for your back and your temper. In the fifty thousand years that man has gardened, nobody has yet designed a convenient spade! There will be certain occasions when a spade is necessary even for the *laissez-faire* gardener, but seldom for digging.

Weeding Apart from a few eccentrics, everyone I know abhors weeding. Sliding a hoe sweetly through a friable April tilth and watching the dark moisture fade away with the weed seedlings, leaving behind neat rows of tender green vegetable plants can be deeply satisfying but more often, the weeds grown faster than you hoped and, try as you might, you never get them all. Conventional lazy persons' gardens are usually designed to inhibit weed growth, but they don't.

Weed-suppressing ground cover has been the obsession of the post-war age. Landscape designers love it – mainly because massed grouping of the same plant reduces the effort they have to make when devising their planting schemes. The theory is that, having cleared the site, rampant species are planted close together to form a carpet through which nothing else will grow. In practice, ground covers often make a wonderful 'nurse crop' under which perennial weeds can become established without your noticing. The apotheosis of ground cover technique was popularised during the 1960s and 1970s when everyone went in for heather beds. 'Why, oh why, can't I grow heather on my limy soil?', was the common wail. Lime tolerant species were sought out and some people even had their topsoil carted away so that they could replace it with peat. Then someone thought of adding conifers. Not handsome pines or larches imitating the heathers' natural companions, but abnormalities of the conifer world. Propagation of any cypress, thuja or juniper that was an odd colour, produced

5

mangled stems or only grew flat became big business and suburban front gardens burgeoned with malformed shrublets that remained unchanged year after year.

Enough of this bigotry! It's unfair of me to impose my subjective tastes on you. *Laissez-faire* gardening can encompass ground cover and indeed, there are parts of the garden where it is the most effective choice. Heathers and conifers too, fit into any *laissez-faire* scheme with comfort – but not to the exclusion of all else. We have to remember the list of 'wants' we itemised earlier; it includes *recreation* meaning that, we must plant for *joy* and not just for weed suppression.

Laissez-faire weeding is not completely trouble-free – weed control never is. Some work is unavoidable but control is possible without compromising the garden and without spending too much time. Later chapters will cover different techniques and you will be able to choose which of these to adopt to suit you own particular style.

Planting One of the big hangovers from the age of Victorian swank is bedding out. Though bedding displays may look fine in our city parks and thoroughfares, there is no place for them in the *laissez-faire* garden. They are labour intensive, horrible in winter and very expensive. There are advantages with bedding – one can ring the changes twice a year, enjoying different colour schemes, for example – but the high labour input fails to produce a big enough return in satisfaction. Bedding plants themselves are quite another matter. Thanks to the extensive research and development that has gone into improving breeds of some tender plants, we are able to choose from a startling range of colours, shapes, sizes and habits. Many of these plants will make important contributions to our *laissez-faire* gardens even though they won't appear in bedding schemes.

Having de-bunked bedding out, only limited planting remains. There will be some to do every year, though this will be enjoyable and can be scheduled to fit in with you, rather than set to a demanding schedule. Again, the text books tell us to plant at a time of year when the number of good gardening days, weather-wise, can be counted on the fingers of a maimed hand. Containerisation has changed all that, enabling planting to fit in with your schedule. Some plants are movable at any time, containerised or not.

Grass care The perfect lawn fanatic will always be with us. He will be out there in a still August dawn, sweeping the dew with his besom so that it soaks into the ground before evaporating. After spreading a series of noxious chemicals on his grass, he'll be deafening you with his range of mechanical equipment all summer and, woe betide anyone who dares to place so much as an explorative toe onto his emerald sward! *Laissez-faire* lawns will not look quite as good as his, but they will be well maintained, healthy and pleasant to walk on, lie on, play croquet over or whatever you have in mind. Further, when you've given a summer bash with fifty energetic guests, you'll be amazed at how quickly your grass recovers. In small gardens, grass may not be necessary at all (see Chapter Ten).

Positive benefits of laissez-faire

Although the technique of *laissez-faire* gardening does not eliminate all the irksome garden chores, it does make them easier and more interesting. In many respects it will *improve* gardens while it *reduces* the work input. In other words, cutting hard work does not necessarily impair the quality of the garden.

We have listed the unpleasant jobs, so now we look at the positive side: garden activities that are universally pleasant and interesting:

Basking and strolling Glancing back at some of the things we *want* from our garden, it is not difficult to see that these can be achieved without more than a minimum of planning. Basking in the sun – well, there'll be plenty of time for that. Strolling among the plants is the keen gardener's main recreation. A friend of mine who is 91 spends most of his time wandering about his magnificent garden armed with secateurs and a little trowel. These he wears in a hip holster, like a horticultural Wyatt Earp. Whenever he sees a weed he digs it. A plant that has become untidy gets a pruning, self-sown seedlings get lifted and replanted in more convenient spots or potted up to be offered to friends – like all genuine plant lovers, he is the very soul of generosity – and all the time, he is just pottering about among his beloved plants, enjoying their presence. At his age, he is unlikely to take on much heavy work, but you'd be surprised at how much he can actually do, without appearing to work at all. Are you getting the idea now? *Laissez-faire* gardening is a way of life rather than merely a technique. Like the Water Rat 'simply messing about in boats', for good gardeners, there is *nothing* – absolutely nothing – half so much worth doing as simply messing about in gardens.

Nature watching This fits into the *laissez-faire* scheme like a hand into a glove. Of late, books and magazines have been overloaded with information about wildlife gardening. Much of it is unhelpful. The more evangelical conservationists would have us turn our gardens into a wilderness of weeds where wild plants and animals could coexist without let or hindrance but where humans are decidedly unwelcome. This, of course, is arrant nonsense. It is quite possible to run an attractive garden with amenity value for humans and at the same time offer a refuge to wild species.

Picking flowers for the house This too, fits in. A common moan against the English – well, a moan from the cut flower industry, anyway – is that we buy each other fewer flowers than any other developed nation. The reason is simple. We *grow* interesting flowers in our gardens and the tradition is to give what we have grown. The same 91-year-old mentioned earlier, fills his cottage with little posies or sizeable branches of anything he wants to observe more closely. Vita Sackville West, who created Sissinghurst, never worked without a little vase of something interesting on her desk. A good habit to mimic. As I write this, on a bitter winter's morning, a fistful of forsythia, picked last week is coming into flower on the windowsill behind me and on my desk, beside the word processor is a small vase of *Cyclamen coum* which, come frost, come snow, flowers from Christmas to April with total disregard. If you adopt the *laissez-faire* approach, you can have all the fun of a garden full of interesting plants without the killing hard work.

Exercise Finally, *gentle* exercise, which can do so much to improve our sense of wellbeing, is part of the gardening scene. We don't have to run a daily marathon, or

7

fight it out on the squash court, but can still stay reasonably fit if we do a little regular gardening.

Thus, after a year or two of *laissez-faire* gardening, you will be fit, well-adjusted, well-rested and your knowledge and understanding of plants will grow from day to day. Like the seventeenth-century poet, Andrew Marvell, you will be amazed at your luck in being able to garden so well with so little effort:

> *What wond'rous Life is this I lead!*
> *Ripe Apples drop about my head;*
> (From 'The Garden', 1681)

Summary

1. *Laissez-faire* gardening eliminates the need for heavy digging and for bedding out

2. Weeding is not eliminated but reduced by various techniques

3. Lawns receive minimal care for optimum health

4. *Laissez-faire* gardening is sympathetic to wildlife

5. Such gardening enables a wide range of plants to be grown without increased work

6. It allows gentle exercise without having to resort to masochistic routines

CHAPTER TWO

Mixed Borders

Borders have been with us since the year dot. Ancient peoples grew their plants in squared-off areas, and according to the garden writer Mayster Ion Gardener (who lived between 1400 and 1440 approximately) – medieval monks produced plants such as saffron crocuses in raised beds 'y-made wel with dyng'.

In more recent times, borders were used for florists' plant collections, for bedding displays and for herbaceous collections. For our purposes, we can define a 'border' as any part of the garden given up to plants. It might be any shape or size and could house practically any set of plants imaginable. One thing is certain: however odd your tastes or whatever style of gardening you finally adopt, you will be certain to have at least one border.

Shape and size

Your first task, as a budding *laissez-faire* gardener, is to clear your mind of any preconceptions. Whatever form you think your borders might take, wipe your mental computer disc and start afresh. Be open minded. Be prepared for anything.

There are no hard and fast rules, but a series of guidelines will help you to obtain optimum results for minimum work input. Remember, in the first chapter of this book, I stressed that *laissez-faire* gardening was *not* work-free. It is highly economical in terms of time, however. The level of time you wish to invest depends on your circumstances and the following advice can be adjusted to suit your specific needs. Flexibility is the key word. Although there is a host of specialist treatments, the ensuing verbiage will be aimed at mixed borders. 'What exactly does he mean by a mixed border?' I hear you ask. The answer: any collection of plants, be they trees, shrubs, herbaceous perennials, annuals, alpines or wildflowers, grown together in some kind of planting scheme. Some, all or only one of these groups may be grown together in any shape, aspect or number.

What sort of results do we want?

Year round interest
Colour

Shape and texture
Character

To these we must always add the list of wants from our first chapter and, since mixed borders are likely to play a major role, we must satisfy as many of those wants as possible. There are also some practical considerations: a mixed border may be positioned to provide shelter or to create a screeen or barrier – either to exclude nosy neighbours or to divide up parts of the garden, increasing the element of surprise. All gardens must be full of surprises. A thrill round every corner to keep the garden stroller interested is an essential part of the designer's art and borders can be arranged in a strategic manner to ensure this. They can also be planted so that the compulsion to walk slowly along their edges, looking for new delights as you go, is irresistible. On top of all this, we must also ensure ideal growing conditions for the plants. Good soil is not an essential ingredient. Judging by the quality of gardening across Britain, there is no connection at all between rich soil and attractive gardens. In fact some of the dullest are found in the rich siltlands of East Anglia where cropping land changes hands at prices that look like telephone numbers. Conversely, superb gardens have been laid out on slag heaps or cliff sides. The secret is to improve the soil as much as possible, to provide the plants with pockets of richness and to grow only those subjects that relish your particular environment.

Climate is more limiting than soil. The worst, by far, is sustained cold. Five weeks of temperatures rising no more than 4°C and plunging below −4°C every night will do far more damage than a single night at −10°C. Most gardens in the colder parts of Europe, in the northern United States and Canada experience worse conditions for overwintering plants than we do in Britain. We all moan about our British climate but for gardening, it could hardly be better. Ireland and Western Scotland probably enjoy the best of our conditions but the problem there is that it never stops raining long enough to allow us to enjoy the plants. Most English handbooks describe gardening in Kent or Devon and assume that the rest of the country must struggle as best they can, ending up with second best. What arrogance! Yorkshire gardeners are among the most skilled in the nation and the choice of magnificent plants that will survive the semi-Siberian conditions of the north-east is enormous. Across the Atlantic, gardeners could grow a far more varied range of plants than they do, even to survive the merciless winters of say, Illinois or Ontario.

The size of the border will depend on several factors but it is important to remember, when *laissez-faire* gardening, that shape and size will exert a great deal of influence on your border management. Certain shapes are awkward; others are difficult to plant effectively. Within the limitations imposed by your overall design, here are some aspects to consider:

Walking on the border soil can be damaging
Curves often result in larger areas than straight sides
Access to the back is important
Sharp angles are difficult to manage
Most borders are more effective if backed by a wall or hedge

Bearing these in mind, it seems logical to avoid too wide a border. If you have to walk all over it to maintain it, your feet will damage the soil structure and maintenance time will increase. It is not possible to state the ideal width because different situations all call for different solutions. My widest border is 11 ft (3.3 m) – far too wide to be easily accessible from one side. A sensible maximum would seem to be about 5 to 6 ft (1.5 to 1.8 m) because much of the area can then be reached with a long-handled implement for most of the time. If a path runs along both sides, the width can be increased, making

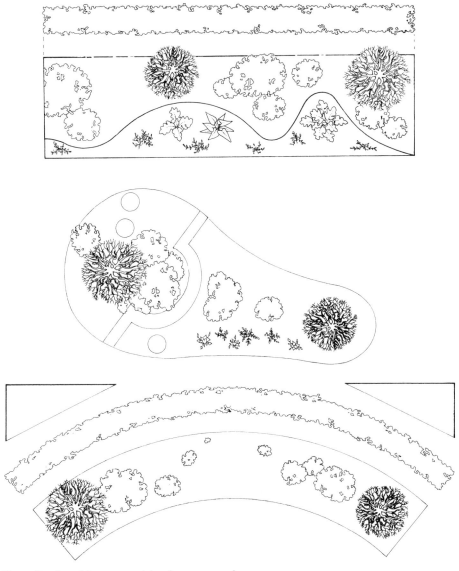

Fig. 1 Borders: Linear type; island type; curved type

room for larger shrubs. Paths are important features in garden design, marking boundaries which divide one area from another and showing the way. They are also functionally important and, though many may be invisible for most of the year, they are nevertheless used during routine maintenance. Thus, a long border running down the length of a hedge or wall, should have a walkway – though this will frequently be lawn – along its front and a secondary gangway along the back. If the border is backed by a wall, you will want a variety of climbing plants along the rear so the path will need to be broken in places to accommodate them, or can be laid between climbers and border. Plants like clematis, will not object to paving slabs over their roots.

Though today's trend is for curvaceous herbaceous, I prefer straight edges. This is merely a matter of personal preference and is not intended to suggest that straight is more tasteful. Anyone who worries about what others see as good or bad taste in his garden is a slave to fashion and should develop a more independent spirit! Do what you like – it's your garden. Because my house was built in the seventeenth century, it seemed appropriate to adopt a little of the symmetry so beloved of gardening in that age. Sissinghurst was also one of the gardens to inspire me in my youth and the first thing I noticed there was that the riotous miscellany of plants was always restrained behind lines, edges and hedges that were, for the most part, straight. From the practical point of view too, I find straight edges easy to look after.

Thicker, block shapes, island beds or circular areas are all suitable for mixed planting. If cutting paths through these is likely to spoil the design, resort to stepping stones. They ensure easy access to most parts of the border and, once the vegetation has grown up, they disappear. The technique of using thin sections of tree trunk as stepping stones has been used at places like Wisley and Rosemoor. The effect is attractive because they are so unobtrusive but there are two disadvantages: they rot

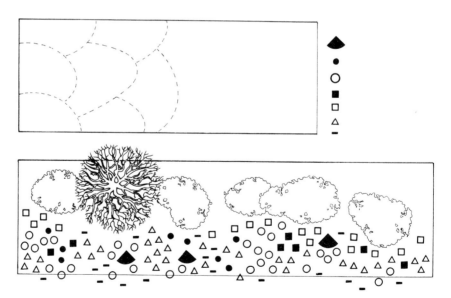

Fig. 2 Mixed borders: Traditional herbaceous plan; *laissez-faire* type

and, in damp winter weather, they become coated with slick green algae making them more deadly than banana skins. When I stated that a garden should be full of surprises – well! One way of preventing this is to stretch a layer of wire mesh over the wood.

Incorporating a prominent feature can be the making of a mixed border. A pond, sitting area, statue or even a sunken rock garden can be surrounded by mixed planting to great effect. All long borders should have at least one focal point and should have a satisfying visual impact from a distance as well as being pleasant to stroll along. Quite a tall order, all that!

Summary

1. Clear your mind of any preconceptions

2. Aim to provide good conditions for plants that suit your soil type and climate

3. Design the border so that you seldom have to walk on the soil

4. Paths at the back are helpful

5. Intersect island beds with paths or provide stepping stones

---

Preparing the ground

At the risk of plodding over old ground, let's assume that you have decided to lay out a new mixed border from scratch. If you already have a thriving garden but want to apply some of the *laissez-faire* principles, all you need to do is take up the advice from the later stage – assuming you did everything necessary to make a perfect border in the first place. You did didn't you?

First, decide on the shape. You may have an existing lawn into which you are cutting the bed. After marking out the area you will need to skim off the turf. Much harder work than it sounds, this, and you will need a spade and half-moon edging tool. Skim as thinly as possible – two reasons for this: first, the more organic matter you can leave behind, the better, and second, there is less heavy turf to cart away. If you wish to use the turf elsewhere, cut it slightly thicker. If not, pile it grass downwards and cover it with a sheet of black polythene. Within a few months, all the grass will be dead and a lovely, humus-rich topsoil will be ready to spread back on the surface of the border.

An alternative is to spray the area off with glyphosate, wait until all the grass is dead and then dig it in. Though less backbreaking than lifting the turf, this method is almost as time consuming and however carefully you spray, there always seems to be a surviving root of bindweed or dock left behind. Clearing a rough, weedy site provides more of a challenge. Eliminating all perennial weeds is essential and can often be done by glyphosate spray. However, you will need several treatments. Even then, a

13

thorough dig through will be necessary and leaving the site fallow for a season will help to ensure clean soil. All this is laborious but the harder you work at the outset, the easier the maintenance will be thereafter.

Having got rid of the last perennial weed, the next task is to take stock of the soil type. If you have no clue about acidity, it will pay you to find out – the level of acidity is expressed as pH. A pH meter can be useful but a good general guide is to peer over as many fences in the neighbourhood as you can and see what kind of plants the others are growing. If you see plenty of camellias, rhododendrons, and lilies, you're in acid country. If clematis and and roses seem to grow especially well and there are no blue hydrangeas, the soil is probably basic. If you can afford a pH meter or a little testing kit, pH 7 is neutral, anything less is acid and anything more alkaline. Many of the more snooty gardeners will tell you that acid soil is necessary for really good gardening. More arrogance! My own soil is strongly alkaline but I still have a vast collection of beautiful and varied plants.

Drainage is discussed more fully later (see Chapter Three), but remember if you are starting from scratch it will pay to ensure that you have adequate drainage in your border. Trouble taken now will save years of frustration later.

Having assessed soil acidity and drainage the next step is to dig. Although I mentioned earlier that you wouldn't need a spade very often, this is one of the few exceptions. Your border will never be dug again so this time you must dig it well. Have a close look at your soil type. If it is excessively light and sandy, dig in as much organic material as you can. A good layer of rotted manure, spread over the site before digging will improve the moisture-retentive properties. Cold clay will benefit from adding compost too and should not be walked on or dug unless dry. Any stones, tramp metal, and general rubbish can be picked off at this time. Dig as deeply as you can, ensuring a thorough incorporation of all the compost or manure. September is the best month for this task. You can then leave the soil untouched while winter frost action prepares a fine tilth for you. In spring you will be burning to get started but resist the temptation to touch the border until the ground has begun to dry and to warm up. In cold areas this won't happen before April but by then you will probably have a green cover of weed seedlings which will be easy to eliminate when you knock the border down to a fine tilth with hoe or rake. You are now ready for planting.

If circumstances compel you to lay your new border out at another time of year, there is no need to wait until September to dig it through. You can prepare the bed at any time, provided the soil is dry enough to work. Corner cutting with motorised cultivators is perfectly acceptable and desirable, provided you dig deep enough to break up the soil a long way down, at least 12 in (30.4 cm). On unstable soils, mechanical cultivating is best done in spring because the powdery tilth can go sour and sad in winter when there is no plant cover. Remember, nothing is better for soil than a thick plant cover.

At spring planting time, a scattering of fertiliser or another layer of mulch will result in rapid establishment. Manure must be well rotted – i.e., crumbly and not excessively smelly – and leaf-mould or compost should be several years old since rotting vegetation can produce acids which are toxic to young plants. This mulch can be applied annually but if that sounds burdensome, a biennial or even triennial treatment will still produce good results. I aim at dressing about half my garden every year but, in practice, seldom manage much more than a quarter.

The stepping stones or paths are best installed early in the project. Once they are there, you can prevent a great deal of soil compaction by using them. Planks of wood laid on the surface also help to reduce pressure from your feet during the preparation of your border.

Summary

1. Plan the shape

2. Skim off turf or eliminate *all* existing vegetation

3. Ensure absence of perennial weeds

4. Check up on drainage and remedy any faults. (See Chapter Three.)

5. Dig deep. Preferably in autumn, or cultivate deeply in spring

6. Level and cultivate the surface until ready for planting

7. Apply the first of regular dressings of mulch and/or fertiliser

8. *Keep off wet soil*

Planting

Up to this point, everything that has been described in the chapter would apply equally to whatever kind of gardening was practised. From now on, the *laissez-faire* technique will be brought into play. Just how well our mixed borders are planted will determine not only how good they will look but also how much time they will demand. The successful garden will marry aesthetic merit with convenience of management. What must we consider, when we choose our plants?

Colour
Shape and texture
Year-round interest
Well behaved plants that need little attention
Covering the ground completely

Colour

Putting colour first was no accident. Of late, bright colours have been frowned upon in some circles. Garden commentators have gone into ecstasy over new varieties with insipid lemon petals or cream foliage but have had to shield their eyes from the

15

awfulness of 'Nonstop' begonias. Dahlias would be as welcome in some gardens as bubonic plague and certain persons of refined taste have been known to remove all flowers from their London Pride because the pink clashes with their colour scheme! But we know better, don't we? After all, we have cleared our minds of any preconceptions. Thus, if dahlias or even those horrendously vulgar Dame Edna gladdies suit our purpose we will jolly well use them, so there!

Shape and texture

Borders have to be composed rather than simply planted up, so shape and texture are at least as crucial as colour. There are so many different shaped leaves, different growth habits and speeds of growth, that the number of possible combinations is almost infinite. Shiny leaves can be as useful to reflect light as white flowers, straight up and down shapes make what garden writers frequently call 'bold statements' – that's to say they stand out. Spreading bushes with horizontal branches give a feeling of breadth at different levels, colourful ground cover perennials can lighten the shadows under shrubs and so on and so on. There is no better way of familiarising yourself with different shapes and textures than by experiencing them in the flesh. Visiting plenty of other gardens – not just National Trust showpieces but gardens of *all kinds* from filling station forecourts to Kew – will generate a wealth of ideas. The famous 'Yellow Book' lists hundreds of private gardens to visit. (Everyone calls it the 'Yellow Book' because it's yellow! It is published annually by the National Gardens Scheme and can be ordered from any bookshop. Its full title is: *Gardens of England and Wales open to the public.*)

You will soon find out what works for you and when you have failures – and we all have plenty of those – don't hesitate to re-plant.

Year-round interest

Vital in every garden, but far more lip service is paid to the concept of year-round interest than actual planting done. Most of us think of the extremes – viburnums for the depths of winter, trees for autumn colour or bulbs for spring. Summer always takes care of itself but what about those awkward intervals? August can be a dreary, tatty month, November is miserable – too soon to get the Christmas spirits out of the drinks cupboard, too late for autumn glory. March always feels as though it's seven weeks long and the spring equinox on the 21st is an ironic and rather nasty joke. But with careful thought, there can be saving graces in the garden, even for these unforgiving months.

One dangerous pitfall for the unwary planter is the 'jam tomorrow' syndrome. The plants in the border are all healthy and thriving, there is plenty of careful positioning so that foliage types harmonise nicely but there never seems to be much going on. Everything looks as though it will be lovely in a week or two. If the flowering time – or the season when some of the plants are especially beautiful – is divided equally between all seasons, there is the danger of never rising above the average. In large gardens, this can be fatal, causing the visitors' eyes to glaze over as they stroll past their fifth tasteful border, set in fractionally different colour schemes but with nothing anywhere to exclaim about. It is desirable to aim for a couple of climaxes. In small gardens, there is no reason why the whole site should not have two or three periods in the year when a crescendo occurs. Though the spaces between star performances may be less spectacular, there is no need for them to be dull; frequently, careful use of perennials can heighten the peaks.

Well behaved plants that need little attention

These are the *only* ones to use. You might have time to crouch over a couple of difficult individuals, especially if you can't bear to be without them, but by and large, you can achieve perfect results with easy subjects. 'Well behaved' means that they will not be too invasive. Your tolerance of invasiveness will depend on the site. In a large border, for example, it may be feasible to underplant with speedy perennials like the pretty-leaved dead nettles *(Lamium maculatum)*. But they do spread at a frightening rate, not only by creeping across the ground but also by seeding freely. In a small border, they could ruin everything. As a general rule, plants with rapidly spreading rootstocks should be regarded with suspicion. Free seeders are less problematic if you have good control of the weeds. The best approach is to make them work for you by seeding in bare areas and filling up the spaces before the weeds colonise them.

As far as shrubs and trees are concerned, the less pruning you have to do, the better. Tree pruning should be limited to removing ugly, damaged or crossed over branches. A minute or so per tree per year should be as much time as you are willing to spare on them. Shrubs needing heavy cutting back – buddleias, for example, are often worthwhile because they are so spectacular in flower but only a few need be grown. The conventional time for pruning spring and early summer flowering shrubs like forsythia or weigela is immediately after flowering. Doing this every year is time consuming and unnecessary. However, an occasional removal of tired old wood helps to keep the plants young and vigorous. The variegated weigela has such good leaf colour that an annual cut to ground level is a technique worth considering. The resulting stems carry larger leaves than normal which, after a long summer of cool cream and green, develop interesting shades at the back end of the year.

Covering the ground completely

This is a vital ingredient for success with *laissez-faire* gardening and could take several years from the first planting of a new border. The composition of the ground-level flora will change over the years as the environment changes. Initially, the young trees and shrubs will provide but little shade and vigorous sun lovers will predominate. As the shade deepens, shade tolerant species will gradually take over, forming their own colonies. The nature of the soil will probably change too, particularly if you are aiming to dress with a mulch every year or so. You need not expect to replant or to rearrange in a radical way – that would take up far too much time. The plants you introduce will tend to determine for themselves how well they are going to colonise. All you do is police the area, making sure the thugs aren't smothering the choice introductions, excluding weed colonies and getting yourself familiar with the whole structure so that, if things aren't going precisely the way you want, you can make some more fundamental changes in autumn or spring. Remember these points and you are well on the way to composing a good *laissez-faire* border.

When it comes to choice of plants, I have three basic house rules which are:

1. Plant only what you like. Don't give a second thought about what the books say – not even this one – or about what our eminent garden designers feel, or what you read in the quality Sunday press. Make up your own mind.
2. Plant only what likes you. You will soon find out what won't grow well for you. If you lose a plant, try one more. If you lose that – grow something else.
3. Grow plants that like each other. Good plant association is essential. Without it, gardens look bitty and unnatural. There is no harm in mixing plants from opposite ends of the earth, provided they share tastes for a similar environment. Plants often get dubbed 'ugly' because of where they are, not how they look.

Now that the guidelines are set, it's time to start considering the choice. Although a rough overall plan is essential, scale drawings showing where every last rootlet is to go are quite unnecessary. Even if you prepare them, the chances are you'll end up with something quite different in a year or two. However, lack of planning could make a lot of hard work, so a deal of forethought is a good investment of your time. Don't sit down with a plan in front of you – go into the garden and stand in front of the border. Walk up and down it, go behind it, squint at it from behind nearby obstacles. What do you see? An area of bare soil? Now do it all again and this time, fill it with imaginary plants. At this stage *do not inhibit your thoughts*. Put anything there – even gnomes – but keep your mind open. If you don't know many plant names, don't worry. Think 'a big bush with gold leaves' or 'something dark and red down there', you can find a plant to match the description later on. Once you have had a couple of brainstorming sessions, either by yourself or with your partner – never mind if it develops into a row; giving birth to an artistic creation is seldom painless – you may want to make some notes and sketches. If you think you have as much as you need stored in your head, and you think it will stay there, forget the sketches altogether.

Everyone should have their own ideas and the following guide can be completely disregarded if you disagree with it. However, there are certain aspects that most successful planting schemes have in common. The first is to create a skeleton. Adding flesh can come later, but the bare bones, because they will consist mainly of trees and shrubs, will be harder to change once they are established.

Trees

Because they are madly expensive, extra care is needed in the selection of trees. They are likely to be the most permanent plants in your garden and there is nothing more frustrating than having a fine tree growing in the wrong place. Where they are to create a canopy over a mixed border, one must consider ultimate size and the amount of shade they will produce. Evergreens throw such dense shade that little will grow under them when they are mature. Conifers and yews are especially bad at this but upright (columnar or fastigiate) varieties throw far less shade. Of deciduous trees, especially in small gardens, much should be demanded. If they flower for three weeks, they must have something to offer for the other forty-nine. The choice of flowering cherries, for example, is very wide but few of them are really good for small sites. Go for varieties that colour well in autumn and have attractive bark. Some get pretty vast – 'Tai Haku', easily the best of the large flowered whites, is far too big for most borders. A smaller white cherry, 'Umineko' is ideal. It grows in a column shape reaching about 8 ft (2.4 m) forms a good, green mass of foliage in high summer and changes to brilliant yellow in autumn. Yet, few garden centres stock it. This brings up another point: good plants are worth searching for but, because most garden centres have disappointingly limited ranges, you should consider visiting specialist nurseries.

Several sorbuses (mountain ashes and whitebeams) are worthy of consideration. Many have pretty blossoms, good winter twigs, jewel-like berries and interesting growing habits. The most compact whitebeam, *Sorbus aria* 'Lutescens', is none the worse for being grown on every corporation landscape. Of the pretty berried varieties, *S. cashmiriana* has pink flowers, white berries and is better grown as a multi-trunked plant rather than as a standard. In sheltered positions, the choice widens: small maples, especially the bolder leaved varieties of *Acer palmatum* and *Acer griseum* earn their keep by providing changing leaf colour or good bark. In mild areas, eucryphias or hoherias will provide magnificent displays to make your friends up in cold limestone country green with envy.

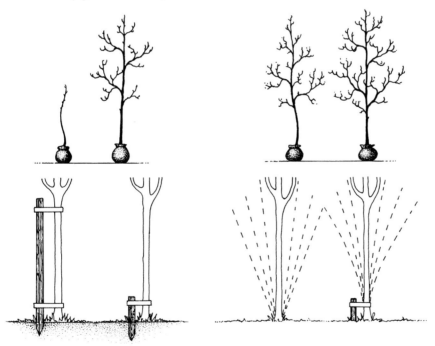

Fig. 3 Planting Trees: Standard or whip?; Staking (a short stake permits stem movement while roots are firmly held)

Evergreens are desirable for mixed borders because they look good in winter and provide their more delicate neighbours with essential shelter. In mild areas, camellias make excellent anchor points but, to be effective, they must be completely healthy, with dark-green, glossy leaves. Up country, where frost and wind make this difficult, hollies come in literally hundreds of different shapes and sizes and some of the cherry laurels are worth considering, especially varieties that flower profusely.

The few examples mentioned here provide the merest glimpse of what trees are available. Getting out and about to observe as many mature specimens as you can will help you to make good choices for your own garden. In a nutshell, the trees in your mixed border will hold things together by providing a skyline and raising the overall height of the planting. In small borders, there may only be room for one or possibly two. Elsewhere, you may decide on a forest of trees with little else – the choice is yours.

When selecting trees, it is not always the best to choose the biggest standards you can find. The larger the tree, the more expensive it is and the less kindly it takes to being moved. Clearly, you will be in a hurry to set up the architectural bits of your planting but, if you can bear to wait a little longer, a smaller tree will always be a better buy. Sometimes, a 'whip' (small sapling without any side branches) will overtake a standard tree in a few years. Always stake standard trees using the low-stake technique. This causes speedy establishment and rapid strengthening of the trunk. The object is for the trunk to flex in the wind while the roots are held motionless in the ground. Aftercare, particularly with standard trees is most important. Water them regularly in their first summer – not with a sprinkle every few days but with a good soak into the ground round their roots every two or three weeks. Even if there has been a certain amount of rain, your new trees are likely to be thirsty. Their root systems will have been damaged on planting and will take a year, possibly two, to recover.

Shrubs

Skilful placing is as important with shrubs as with trees. With them, you can separate off sections of the border, creating little bays and pockets which offer sheltered spots for the herbaceous plants. You can mimic natural woodland by providing an underbrush of woody subjects to hide the boles of your trees. You can even adopt a semi-formal approach and use hedging plants to clip into obelisks, pyramids or balls. Ground rules with shrubs are much the same as with the trees. They must pull their weight and must be trouble free. If you have reservations about too much bright colour, go for subtle leaf tones. Conversely, if you want some good splashes from time to time, select flowering species and go for the varieties you like best. Different compositions suit different gardens. One warning note: a mix of variegated foliage grown close together can look horribly bilious. Foliage contrasts are desirable too, but are more effective if carried out with restraint against the natural background colour – green.

1. Bold planting of perennials in mixed
   borders.

2. A boldly planted edge, chives used here,
   can 'bind' loose planting together.

Herbaceous zone

Having placed the trees and shrubs as you want them, next, think about the non-woody flora. Recent fashion has tended to shove herbaceous plants into a secondary role, relying on shrubs and trees to provide most of the interest and merely to plant ground-cover material to suppress weeds at their feet. This attitude not only shows poverty of imagination but can ruin an otherwise pleasant garden. Herbaceous plants, especially in cold parts of the world, are responsible for most of the change in the season. Think of the traditional herbaceous border. In winter it was dull and brown, all clipped back and tidied away with nothing to enjoy before the first crown imperial in April. But oh, that summer display! Plants, richly fed and well tended, would grow an inch or more a day and in their season flood the garden with colour – scarlet poppies and blue lupins in June, with mallows, bellflowers and delphiniums in high summer and a climax of Michaelmas daisies in autumn. Some devoted gardeners persevere with such borders today but, *laissez-faire* they are not! What we have to do is to take as many of those plants as will transfer and add them to our mixed borders. There are far too many to discuss in detail but the general principles apply to so many. It pays to avoid:

Florists' types and fancy hybrids
Anything in need of staking or tying
Plants easily smothered

The Plant List will provide you with a good ground list but please don't think it in any way comprehensive. 'Florist' doesn't mean from a flower shop – but something so highly bred as to bear little resemblance to its wild forebear. Pot hyacinths, 'Pacific Giant' delphiniums, large colourful phloxes and mop head chrysanthemums are all examples. Planted among the foliage they look out of place – as if someone had shoved in a plastic flower or two to jazz things up. They also dislike growing in anything but optimum conditions.

The reasons for not staking or supporting plants are obvious – time's money. But, lax plants such as the herbaceous *Clematis* × *jouiniana* can be charming if they are pleached through supporting shrubs. It is important to plant them a reasonable distance away from their host plant at first so they do not compete for the same

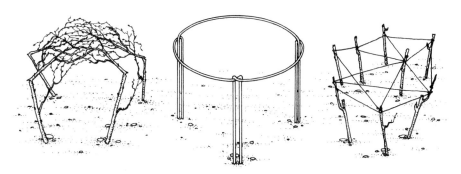

Fig. 4 Supports: Peasticks; metal hoops; sticks and strings

nutrients. Remember, left on their own, plants grow towards light or head south, so plant them on the dark side of the host shrub. Sometimes, you will have to pull young leads into the host but this is a trifling job. Other examples of plants happy to grow like this are *Clematis × durandii, C. integrifolia* and several of the perennial sweet peas. I am especially fond of the brick-red *Lathyrus rotundifolius*, a Persian native whose seeds are diamond hard and more pigheaded about germinating than any of its relatives.

Since you won't have time to mollycoddle anything, plants likely to be swamped out of existence are best avoided, particularly deep in the border. Life at the border front is a different matter and here, because they are so easy to get at, a few of the more niggly plants can be accommodated. New introductions can be tried near the front where you can keep an eye on them for a season before deciding whether they are suitable for you and where their final homes should be.

Now that you have a broad impression of the general principles, you should be able to interpret them to your own particular situation. At first, unless you purchase extravagantly, your border will be scanty. A few hints on *laissez-faire* propagation follow to help you bulk up your plants quickly and cheaply. There is no need to keep the perennials in discrete groups. Let them merge so that the overall effect is more like a piece of wild flora than a contrived border.

Summary

1. Plant for colour, shape, texture and year-round interest

2. Use plants that don't need too much attention

3. Aim to cover the ground completely

4. Plan for several climaxes each year – not a twelve-month compromise

5. Select trees which offer more than just a short flowering season

6. Avoid too much fancy foliage colour. The main colour should be green

7. Be sure to include some evergreens in the planting scheme

8. Herbaceous plants are *vital*. Have plenty

9. Watch tree aftercare – the bigger the tree the more the care needed

Finally, remember the three rules: Plant what you like. Plant what likes you. Use plants that like each other.

Propagation hints

Traditional textbooks are full of helpful information on how to propagate perennials. Most of it is sound and useful. Taking matters beyond these classic rules, in the *laissez-faire* garden there are several handy shortcuts which I have found successful and rewarding in terms of time saving and speedy results.

Most perennials will split. The more hilarious guides show you, usually with pictures, how to use two forks for this. You lift a clump of, say Michaelmas daisy, plunge two garden forks in back to back and tease the plants apart. The result is two smaller lumps, lots of little broken off bits – many with little roots on them – and a whole mess of soil, usually on your best lawn. With congested lumps the results are more dramatic – a broken fork handle. It's always your neighbour's fork that breaks, the one that had belonged to her great aunt who was given it by one of the Buckingham Palace gardeners in 1923. In the *laissez-faire* garden you haven't time for this much painstaking activity. Simply fork a small part of the plant up, and tear this into individual pieces. Each piece should have at least one shoot visible – but no more than three – and a little root. If the lump is badly congested, try cutting into it with a trowel or even a Stanley knife. Then, plunge these pieces into the ground a few inches apart – nearly all will take and result in youthful plants. Meanwhile, the original parent is still *in situ*, undisturbed. The result is a spread of plants rather than a rigid group. I am not sure who started the extraordinary idea of always planting in threes. Plant as many or as few as you like. Four, six, two, it makes little difference in the long run because your border will be a total cover, not a connected series of groups.

As an insurance policy and to further the natural look, some of the pieces you break off could be pushed in elsewhere in the garden. If you belong to a garden society or have like-minded friends, the same bits can be potted up to produce containerised plants. Potted this way in March, they will produce a rootstock rapidly and be 'market size' plants by the end of spring. If surplus material still remains after that, throw it away. You haven't time to cherish unwanted pots of plants which will end up on the heap anyway. Although spring and autumn are the best times to split the plants, many perennials are amenable to the treatment at other times of the year. Spring flowering primulas should be divided during the first damp spell after flowering. You must be ruthless with these – literally tear them to bits and plant the bits. They will look miserable for a month afterwards but will flower profusely the following spring. The earlier after flowering they are split, the better they will flower next year.

If some of the plants are self-seeding less effectively than you think they should, make a point of saving some seed to beef up the population. Hints on seed collection are given later. (See Chapter Five.)

Cuttings are also feasible without overdoing the time input but all propagation requires a certain amount of time. Because yours is limited, it is perhaps best to limit the taking of cuttings to those plants which are short-lived and expensive to replace, and of course, to plants which are relatively easy to root. This would include penstemons, pinks, lavenders, perennial wallflowers and some of the silver-leaved shrubs. The most expensive method is also the most foolproof – mist propagation. Next best is to invest in a small electric propagation unit or even a cheap windowsill

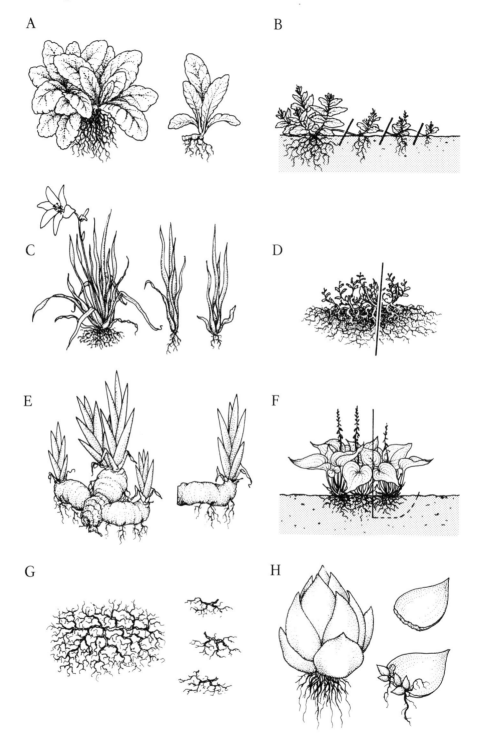

propagator. These merely provide 'bottom heat' to the soil to promote rapid rooting. If even that seems too elaborate, you can resort to plunging the cuttings in a sharp sand/peat mix in a cool, sheltered coldframe in July. The latter system is slow and not fully reliable but it does leave the cuttings to strike roots without much supervision, enabling you to concentrate on other things. The same frame can be used for woody cuttings in winter. A large number of shrubs will strike from slips of young but mature growth inserted into a gritty mix. Willows and poplars are the easiest but there are plenty of other valuable woody plants that will propagate this way – even some of the evergreens.

Root cuttings are fiddly but quite easy, particularly with plants that have thick, fleshy tissue. *Crambe cordifolia*, a giant cabbage required in every garden for its great tidal wave of pearly blossoms in June, can be grown by burying 6 in (15.2 cm) lengths of root in good soil. Oriental poppies, catananche, dicentras and echinops (globe thistle) are all easy from root cuttings trimmed to the length of cigarettes and set on their sides in seed trays, full of sandy compost.

If the idea of all this heavy propagation palls, don't do it. Your garden will go on quite happily without but, since you will have time and will be enjoying the garden so much by now, you may want something extra to do.

Summary

1. Splitting is the simplest way to multiply perennials

2. Split down to the smallest piece, provided at least one shoot and some roots remain

3. Cuttings of soft (non-woody) material are best taken in July

4. Hard cuttings (woody) can be taken between October and March

5. Root cuttings are not difficult

Fig. 5 Propagation
A Division (Primula): divide into single rosettes
B Creeping Perennials: split off individual shoots with roots
C Clumpy Perennials (Day Lily): split individual shoots
D Matted root stock (Aster): slice with knife or chop with spade
E Rhizome (Iris): cut away old rhizome and slice new into individual shooting pieces
F Tough roots (Hosta): use spade to slice out part of root stock
G Fragile root systems: lift plant when dormant, tease roots apart
H Lily: take scale leaves

CHAPTER THREE

Gardening on Gravel

Gravel and good gardening go hand-in-hand. It suits the *laissez-faire* approach and saves vast quantities of time.

Advantages

The beauty of gravel lies in its versatility. You can walk on it, plant in it, use it to cover a weed-proof plastic film, use it as a permanent mulch or simply surface your car parking area with it. If your artistry outweighs your love of plants, you can go Japanese and rake patterns in it, placing the occasional rock or obelisk here and there to fight off boredom. On the other hand, the most manic plant collector can effect some sort of cohesion in his design by creating a roughly uniform surface – gravel helps here because it conceals what goes on underneath, enabling the plants to receive their different special treatments.

Here are some more advantages:

Variety

Gravel comes in all shapes, sizes and colours from fine granite grit, suitable for little rocky screes, to large flinty cobbles which can be hell to walk on unless carefully laid. Colours run from stark white – mainly for Japanese enthusiasts again – through the pinkish shades of the Devon granites, the honey of limestone shingle to dark basalt. Hardness, texture and colour depend on the minerals that make up the stone. The choice is enormous.

Natural

Gravel is natural. Much of it has been made over aeons by ice or water grinding rock down, wearing away the edges, smoothing surfaces. Because it occurs so commonly in nature, gravel seems to be less alien to gardens than almost any other landscape material, even when every pebble has been placed artificially.

Cheap

When natural hewn stone costs an arm and a leg, and concrete slabs are both expensive and unsightly, gravel comes cheap at a few pounds per ton. The only costly part is the transport.

Easy

Gravel is easy to install. All you need is a wheelbarrow and a friend.

Time saving

Above all for the clock-watcher, gravel provides huge opportunities for time saving without detracting from the garden. Indeed, it is one of the few truly labour-saving materials that actually enhances the environment.

A less tangible advantage is that it makes an excellent design aid. It provides a perfect medium where plants are allowed to spill over from borders and take root in paths, softening the line at the edges. Conversely, where it is contained, gravel makes a hard contrast between boundaries at the edge of a lawn or border, beside a stone terrace, or separating a pool area from another section of the garden.

Disadvantages

Though few, there are disadvantages and they must not be dismissed. The biggest drawback with gravel is that once laid down, the stuff is almost impossible to remove. On friable land, over a short period, a melange of shingly loam develops between gravel mulch and soil proper. Although it might be feasible to scrape a fair proportion from the top, a good deal is bound to be left behind. Over rough surfaces, the task of removal is even more difficult and laborious. So, think very carefully about where the gravel is to be laid and, once down, consider it a permanent geological feature.

Keeping gravel within bounds can pose problems. A single pea-sized pebble in the wrong place can ruin the adjustments on a cylinder lawnmower. The sound and feel of walking on a stone terrace that has a sprinkling of pebbles grinding between shoe sole and stone surface is more excruciating than a chorus of angle grinders. However, most of these problems are easily prevented and the few disadvantages are so heavily outweighed by points in favour that gravel gardening should, and no doubt will, become an important part of every discerning gardener's programme.

Preparing the ground

Areas where gravel can become an integral part of the garden structure are so diverse that laying down a set of ground rules here seems rather pointless. However, there are certain principles which must be adhered to, wherever the gravel is to be laid. First, since once down little can be done to change things, it is essential that whatever is needed beneath the surface be there before the stones are spread.

Drainage

Drainage is the first consideration. Very few modern gardens have proper drainage schemes installed. Most of us merely rely on natural falls and soil porosity to get rid of surplus water. We soon get to know where the soggy bits are, and tend to plant accordingly. The idea that a layer of shingle on the surface of a growing area will enhance drainage is fallacious. What gravel does is to keep the *necks* of the plants – that portion where the stem stops and the root starts – dry in winter. This can mean the difference between life and death with some species but, however dry at the surface, few plants will survive with their roots permanently in stagnant water. If your soil is naturally free draining, no action need be taken but if you suspect that waterlogging might become a problem, installing a simple drain or two is easier than you think. The quickest way to assess a given area is to see how long it takes for surface water, after a particularly heavy rain, to soak away. Small pools of water sitting on the surface – technically known as 'puddles' – are a bad sign. If they remain more than a few hours after the rain has stopped, you have a drainage problem.

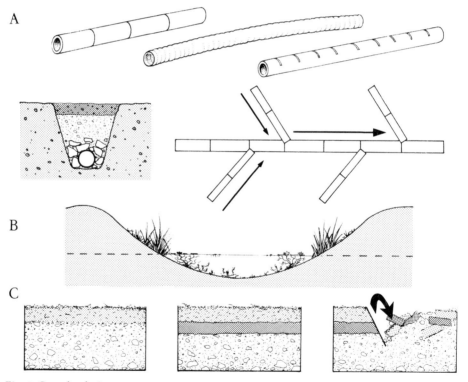

Fig. 6 Gravel – drainage
A Various drain types: clay pipes, plastic pipes (section and plan)
B Water table—create a pond
C Good soil structure; bad soil structure; breaking down a compacted soil pan

If you happen to be on friendly terms with any farmers or drainage contractors, they may be able to sell you a few clay tiles or a length of plastic draining pipe. They frequently have small quantities left over from field drainage schemes. The plastic pipe has holes, the principle being that water seeps in from the soil and runs along its length to an outfall. A trench for such pipes need not be very deep – 18 in (45.7 cm) is plenty – and the pipes should be sloped to carry water away to where it can run off without being a nuisance. A single pipe may be all you need, but in a problem area it might pay to install a herringbone system.

A very crude alternative, if piping seems unduly laborious to you, is to dig out the soil of a wet patch and replace about half the volume with coarse rubble. This can provide a small local improvement to drainage immediately above the rubble. It may also reduce the fertility of the soil there – not necessarily a disadvantage, particularly where gravel gardening is to become a way of life.

A chronically wet patch, one that seems to stay soggy even in a dry summer, may be caused by a natural spring or high water table. The obvious choice here is to snatch an advantage from the adversity and enhance the wetness, using the site for moisture loving plants. Dig here, and you might even be lucky enough to create a natural pond – riches indeed while the rest of us struggle with horrible butyl liners and agonise over correct levels. The idea is for the gravel layer to continue down the sides and under the water surface. Pushing aquatics into thick shingle is simplicity itself and their anchoring roots develop with surprising speed. Artificially boggy areas can be created by removing a foot or so of topsoil and laying plastic sheeting – preferably several thicknesses – before replacing the soil. If the sheeting is laid in a dish shape, water will collect at the centre but is unlikely to result in a very long lasting pond because of seepage – the overlying soil can act as a syphon. However, a wet area looks more natural if it slopes down to a soggy centre and the resulting puddle can be topped up with a (licensed) hose from time to time if the rains fail for more than a week or two.

Soil structure

If the gravel is to be used purely as a mulch over ordinary soil, the opportunity to improve soil structure, texture and humus level will never occur again. Composts, manure or any other form of 'improver' will be out of the question once the gravel has been laid. Thus heavy, hungry or exceptionally thin soils will benefit from a rich dressing of manure or other fibrous organic material. Once the gravel is down, the ground beneath will have become, effectively, subsoil and you will have relinquished the power to be able to do much more to it without an enormous upheaval.

Soil structure is a fragile thing. Cavorting about in heavy boots on a wet surface can reduce some of our less stable soils to putty which will set to ferroconcrete when it dries. Wheeling barrows of gravel across it will make matters worse but because the newly-laid surface looks so nice and neat, it's all too easy to forget the destruction you are wreaking underneath. The cure? None! The prevention: work only when the ground is dry and soil crumbly. Even then, it pays to lay planks down where possible to reduce pressure from your feet or the wheels of your barrow. A good rule, when gardening anywhere in a damp season is to tell yourself that surfaces where plants are growing are really layers of thin ice overlying a bottomless chasm. Tread lightly – your life depends on it – and tread only where absolutely necessary. For instance, if you leave a rake on the border, don't walk back on to collect it – hook the handle towards you with a stick or another tool. This advice may seem footling but, because your *time* is at a premium, the less you have to do to your soil, the better. Keeping off it will help ensure minimum tillage.

Special conditions

If you intend to use gravel for plants needing special conditions at root level, those conditions must be provided before the gravel is set down. One of my scree terraces has clematis and honeysuckle on the south facing wall at the back, where they thrive against all odds – but more of that later (see Chapter Eight) – and drought loving sedums in front. The knack was to provide deep, rich soil for the climbers but to lay rubble and larger pebbles in front for the hot-dry lovers. Actually the rubble was already there and, being bone idle, I merely spread pea shingle over the whole lot – concrete, rubble and deep loam – and followed up with a planting scheme that tied in with what I knew to be the substrata.

Besides plants, other features will need careful thought. If plants or walkways are planned, these will need extra reinforcement under the surface. Larger stones or hardcore can be tamped down where people are likely to tread. This serves a double purpose: not only does it enable the ground to withstand the extra wear caused by passing feet, it also inhibits plant growth over the paths without preventing it completely. This results in a much more naturalistic effect than having, say, a neatly bordered brick pathway or anything worse such as concrete. Water pipes or electric cables, laid to supply ponds or lighting, must be buried deep enough and protected from possible damage by sharp edges of large rubble or an inadvertent jab with the spade.

Weeds

Finally, because they can ruin everything, it is essential that all perennial weeds are completely eradicated before the gravel goes down. Control afterwards is difficult and time consuming, even when chemicals are used, so if any of the big enemies are there, they must be dealt with. The worst weeds are, in no particular order of beastliness, stinging nettles, bindweed, ground elder, creeping buttercup, willowherb – all varieties – creeping cinquefoil and couch. If a single seedling of any of these is present, be sure not to lay the gravel, even if it means being held up for a whole season.

Laying gravel

Having prepared the ground, the mechanics of laying the gravel are simple but laborious. Gravel is heavy so you will need a sturdy builder's wheelbarrow with a loop of steel running round in front of the wheel to facilitate tipping. Clearly, the nearer the gravel lorry can shoot its load, the less distance you have to cart the stuff. The first mistake is usually to overfill the barrow. Many small loads, distributed evenly will make spreading and raking less arduous than trying to barrow too much at once. A stout, steel rake is essential and a roadmender's shovel a great help, though, at a pinch, one can make do with a spade. Then, having dumped the heaps, just spread it about until reasonably even.

Thickness of the layer depends on the kind of gravel used and what goes on underneath. Over rich loam, the mulch should be at least $2\frac{1}{2}$ in (6.3 cm) thick and if you err, go thicker to prevent soil breaking through. On existing gravelly or stony ground, a thinner layer will suffice. If, after a year or so, the level has eroded and soil is showing here and there, fresh gravel can be added to top up. However, if the original layer was thick enough it should last for ever.

Clearly, much of the work decribed so far is heavy and laborious. But it is all 'one off' and when completed, your life will become easier. The results, both visual and from the time saving point of view, will delight you – let's hope!

Summary

1. Ensure adequate drainage

2. Build up diminished soil humus by adding rotted manure, compost or grass

3. Guard against damage to soil structure by trampling

4. Provide any special conditions needed for particular plants or pathways, etc

5. Eliminate all perennial weeds before laying a single pebble

The choice

Choice is largely a matter of taste. When choosing gravels, four points must be borne in mind:

1. What will look best?
2. What will suit the plants?
3. What is the function of the gravel layer?
4. Make your calculations in metric. Gravel is graded metrically these days. (For this reason the following section does not show imperial measurements.)

Different gravels produce different results. For mulches, a fine pea-sized grit is best. This is better at keeping in moisture than larger stones and is easier to weed. For pathways a mixture can be used – not necessarily blended but laid in runs of different sizes to imitate a typical mountain scree or dry stream bed where, it seems, pebbles of similar sizes tend to congregate together.

The visual point of view is easily dealt with: choose what *you* like best. All the dictates of garden magazines, landscaping experts and helpful neighbours are to be ignored if they run counter to your personal tastes. A good ground rule is to avoid exotic material and go for a local source. A friend of mine in Lincolnshire, went to enormous expense to surround his new swimming pool with special slate brought up from Cornwall. The result was unnatural-looking and at odds with his house, built of warmly coloured local limestone. In Devon, Cornwall and parts of Scotland, granite occurs naturally and comes in some interesting shades. Gravel from these regions suits the acid-loving plants grown in so many western gardens.

Cornwall also produces a useful, silver-grey grit – a by-product of the china clay industry – which is too fine to be called gravel but makes an excellent base and seems to stimulate vigorous root growth. Almost every county of Britain has its own supply of gravel, though locating the source is not always easy. Most quarry firms offer ranges of size or grade and prices vary according to demand and supply, though there is seldom much difference between the cost of large pebbles or pea grit.

Most deliveries are quoted in 5 tonne or 10 tonne loads. Garden centres and builders' merchants are best avoided as they will be taking a 'middle-man's' profit and the resulting price will be high. However, where very small quantities of special grit are needed, these are often available bagged in 50 kg sacks. Insoluble poultry grit can be bought from animal feed merchants and makes excellent sharp material for blending in composts as well as laying down with larger gravels. For bigger stones, some quarries have unwanted grades which are inexpensive. Remember, the bigger the pebble, the more difficult it is to walk on and to weed.

A tonne sounds an awful lot but gravel weighs heavy and is better laid too thick than too thin. On average, each tonne, if laid to a depth of about 50 mm will cover an area of about 17 sq m. Thus, a level area of, say, 34 sq m would need at least two tonnes.

The practical properties of gravel are rooted in its function as a mulch. Soil beneath the layer stays moist longer while the gravel itself drains and dries quickly. In practical terms this means that plants regarded as tender or difficult to over-winter can often be brought through periods of frost and extreme wet. The same plants in conventional borders will die with depressing regularity every winter. In my own cold, windy garden, *Salvia patens, Cosmos atrosanguinea* and *Acidanthera mureliae* have all survived for years under a pea gravel blanket but fail every winter elsewhere in the garden. In 1986 they survived a frost of −16°C and still, to everyone's utter amazement, the salvias thrust through the campanulas I had planted, assuming them to be dead, and flowered from late summer onwards. For clock-watchers, this feature widens the scope for interesting plants without having to worry about rooting cuttings or lifting to over-winter.

Where gravel is used specifically for paths or car parking areas, it must be remembered that pea size is very unpleasant to walk on if it is too deep. For that purpose a size of 10 mm, 14 mm or 20 mm is more practicable, even though most plants grow better in pea gravel (4 mm to 6 mm).

It is equally important, especially in the *laissez-faire* garden to remember that

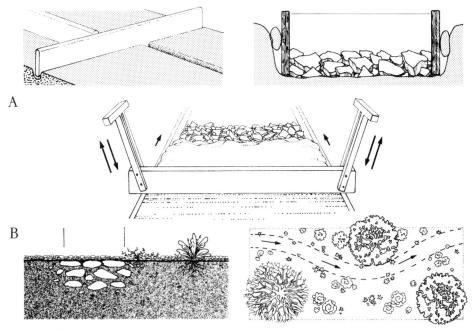

Fig. 7 Making a concrete path
A Plan; section; screeding
B Invisible path in gravel (section and plan)

boundaries are merely notional. The idea that paths and drives are exclusively for thoroughfares, not for plants, must be driven out of your head! In a good garden, plants are welcome everywhere and where space is limited, planting up every centimetre is doubly important. At the same time, it is essential to delineate, to a certain extent, to prevent visitors from parking on the plants and to prevent paths from becoming completely overgrown.

A useful way round the problem of walking in pea gravel – you should try it in open-toed sandals! – is to lay a series of stepping stones down the centre of the path. To keep them free of pebbles, they should stick up at least 25 mm from the surface and be laid firmly so they do not teeter when stepped on. Having, as my wife tells me, legs up to my armpits, I tend to lay these too far apart for people who are less able to 'stride the earth like a very colossus'. The gap between slabs should never be more than about 0.3 m. As well as being more pleasant to walk on, stepping stones point out the route people are expected to take. Without them, a large gravelly area may appear to the uninitiated to be fair game to wander over at will – irritating if you have just planted a crop of baby plants or have newly emerging bulbs which they can't hear being squashed for the noise of their feet crunching in the gravel.

If you can't run to natural stone and dislike buying concrete slabs, it is not difficult to make your own. A wooden mould is easy to make for square blocks but disc-shaped stepping stones are more interesting, even though they look a bit raw for the first

33

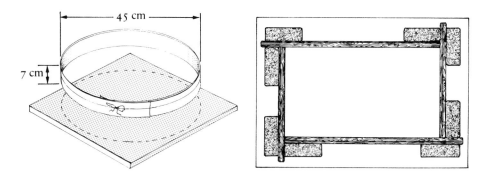

Fig. 8 Making circular and rectangular paving slabs in concrete

couple of seasons. The mould can be made from any ribbon of metal about 7 cm deep and long enough to shape into a ring at least 45 cm in diameter. (An old 40 gallon (200 litre) drum, sliced to size, is ideal.)

Use a stiffish mix (1 part cement to 4 parts sand/gravel mix) and place the mould on rough planking to ensure a non-slip surface. Weldmesh, or even old scraps of metal embedded into the discs will increase their strength. If the stones fail to deter people from wandering over the 'growing' areas, it may be necessary to place a few strategic plants to bar their way. Thorny ones are best but if they fail, the only alternative is to lay a minefield!

Ornamentation of the gravel garden is a little different from ornamentation elsewhere. To enhance the feeling of a dry river bed, large boulders can be effective. The bigger the better but those that have been rounded by the action of the water are more harmonious than disembodied lumps of quarried stone. One of my terraces has a great hernia-causing lump of tufa which looks reasonably natural and is a useful repository for small saxifrages and alpine primulas. Gravel gardens are good to sit in because the smells of the aromatic plants rise well when the stones are hot but seats should be set on firm bases to prevent their legs from sinking in.

Summary

1. Decide what size gravel to use: small for mulch, larger for paths, largest for heavy wear

2. Use a local source. Deal with the quarry if possible

3. Consider stepping stones to mark pathways and to facilitate walking

4. Try to arrange for seating in the midst of the gravel garden

5. Quantity: 1 tonne will provide a 50 mm thick layer over an area of about 17 sq m

Planting

Though mulches are supposed to inhibit weed seedlings, pea gravel fails in this respect. However, on the plus side, it seems to act as a positive stimulus for many species shy to seed elsewhere. Certain conifers self-seed, so do penstemons, shrubby euphorbias, clematis, roses and a host of small bulbs. Pricking out is simplicity itself – just tug gently, and the whole plant lifts from the gravel. This is where the labour-saving aspect is so manifest. There are two approaches. The true *laissez-faire* gardener will tend to allow anarchy in his scree. An occasional gloss over, pulling any obvious weeds, is essential at least before they set seed, but other than thinning congested progeny, the technique is to leave well alone and may the best man win! Planting may seem haphazard but careful control of colour and shape will prevent the whole area degenerating into a plantsman's mess. Obvious colour clashes can be avoided at planting time but where colonies of the wrong plant are developing at the expense of anything choice or delicate, simply remove enough of the offending plant to give the others an unfair advantage. Heavy work comes no more than once a year, when a major tidy-up is essential. At that time, slow multipliers can be bulked up by splitting using the same technique as already described (see Chapter Two).

If you feel a little more control is essential, then areas of gravel can be kept pure with a hoe. Temptation to use herbicide here should be resisted because hoeing is so quick and simple that chemical treatments offer little advantage. The horizontal blade is best because it leaves the gravel undisturbed. I have sworn by Wilkinson's 'Swoe' which can even be operated one handed in easy going. The action of the Swoe is normally to slice the weed just above the roots. In pea shingle, weeds are often pulled – or pushed – below the surface by the action of the Swoe. If they are left on top, collecting them up is quite unnecessary. Unless it rains for a week, they will shrivel and disappear without disfiguring the display. Clearly, where gravel is to be left part bare, the planting must be done in groups with uncontrolled spread prevented. The appearance of this kind of scheme is quite different from the wild look of the first but, if anything, weed control and maintenance is slightly easier. Group planting needs careful planning and positioning to avoid ugly little bunches or ill-designed wodges. Different types of foliage make for useful contrasts and 'feature' plants need to anchor down each group.

The number of plants that thrive in gravel is so vast that it is quite impossible to list them comprehensively. To whet your appetite, here are some examples of situations where gravel has worked well . . .

In a garden

I once visited a garden with a hot dry area, about 8 ft (2.4 m) wide, 30 ft (9.1 m) long and running along the side of a swimming pool enclosure. Nothing could have been less natural than the stark white walls, the dazzle of the sun on the water and the heat from the paving. Containers had been dotted about on the flagstones in front and planted with strong coloured summer bedding – petunias, pelargoniums and begonias. The 30 ft (9.1 m) bed was covered with gravel which varied in size but was topped with a liberal sprinkling of smooth stones and boulders, the largest some 2 ft (0.6 m) across, which were so hot in the sun one could hardly bear to touch them. Amongst this stony desert was planted a collection of spiky, arid loving plants: *Carex buchananii*, a russet-coloured sedge with whippy leaves was here, so was the gold striped bamboo (*Arundinaria viridistriata*), dark green stemmed *Genista* 'Lydia' and one or two stocky silver plants like *Artemisia absinthium, Anthemis cupaneana* and *Helichrysum splendidum*. At the back, taller phormiums grew with a selection of cypresses chosen for the darkness of their foliage. Planting was sparse – lots of space between each subject – and weeds controlled with an occasional spray of paraquat between the plants. The effect was of a piece of arid Australia, making a striking contrast with the cool blue of the pool.

On a terrace

A terrace about 15 ft (4.5 m) by 30 ft (9.1 m) overlying poor, stony, soil, exposed to all weathers but well-lit. Pea gravel was used throughout and small paving slabs set in a serpentine pattern through the centre. Soil beneath varied from stiff clay to free-draining limestone brash – very alkaline. The area lies between the front of my house and a formal – well, formalish – sunken garden which is divided up into a series of rectangles. It seemed appropriate to insist on a modicum of discipline among the plants here where a concentration of dwarf bearded irises and helianthemums makes up the main body of the planting scheme. These were placed in loose groups but allowed to expand to merging point. Many of the different red helianthemums clash horribly with their neighbours so careful siting is essential. The double scarlet 'Mrs Earle' is a particular offender but lasts so long and flowers so faithfully that one has to forgive her tartiness. Among dwarf bearded irises, some of the more exquisite varieties will multiply well but only produce a handful of blooms. Gravel, dry feet and direct sunlight help to keep this problem at bay for all varieties seem to flower better in stones than anywhere else. The intermediate cultivars 'The Bride' and 'Atroviolacea' flower furiously and look striking together. Shorter varieties come in all shades – my favourite blue 'Austrian Skies' performs well and of the brownish shades, 'Little Bill' is one of the most intriguing because of the delightful contrast between the bright blue beard and beige petals. 'Ruby Contrast' has similar blue beards which show up against deep garnet – almost black – petals.

By the time the helianthemums have started to flower, the dwarf irises are over but provide useful sword-like foliage to set off the sprawling habits of the rockroses. Other plants on this terrace are of similar stature to the main performers. Near the edges, *Alchemilla conjuncta* – much better behaved than *A. Mollis* which seeds with total incontinence – merges with stubby, non-climbing ivy, the grey backed *Osteospermum* 'Paleface' and *Erodium chrysanthum*. (*Alchemilla conjuncta* is often sold under the name *A. Alpina* – quite wrongly, but the two species are superficially similar.) London pride adores gravel, staying small and compact in hard ground, as does culinary sage which is grown here as much for the flowers as for the scented foliage. An occasional large hellebore – *H. corsicus* is least bothered about full light – gives plenty of relief

3. A terrace planted with sage,
   Osteospermum 'Weetwood' and
   helianthemums.

4. One of the author's gravel gardens.

5. A well developed shrubby border with
varying foliage highlighted by the
golden hop *Humulus* 'Aurea'.

6. Laced pink 'Valerie Finnis' with dark
foliaged sedum 'Bertram 'Anderson' on
pea gravel

from winter dullness, flowering at the same time as early crocus species and *Cyclamen coum*.

On a less formal terrace

Elsewhere in my garden is a far less formal terrace which has been left to its own devices – the full *laissez-faire* technique. It would be quite untrue to say that it requires no attention, but it is only fractionally more demanding than a ground cover of mixed heathers and is so very much more interesting and rewarding. Originally, the intention had been to grow groups of plants with relatively large spaces in between, as with the more formal area just described. In practice, after a couple of seasons, the plants seem to have developed their own ideas about where they want to grow and I, well, let's face it, have lost control.

Certain species have been troublesome, threatening the livelihood of everything else. *Kentranthus ruber*, an indispensable garden plant, far too readily despised because of its commonness, is a thug on gravel where its great taproots go down about 1 ft (0.3 m) and defy destruction. Some of the sisyrinchiums get a bit bossy: *S. striatum* seeds too prolifically but is striking enough to include, despite the miserably short flowering season and disgusting black foliage in a frosty winter. The smaller *Sisyrinchium bermudianum* is easily the best of the blues, flowering for ever. There is a jolly buff-flowered form sold to me originally as 'Biscutellum' but often known as 'Quaint and Queer' (rather too gay a name for me) which goes very well with the true blue. Though sterile, this plant is a nurseryman's dream, splitting easily. Indeed, most of the small sisyrinchiums are more floriferous, if split several times a season.

In a shaded area

Though associated with hot, dry conditions it would be quite wrong not to consider gravel as a possible medium for a cool, shaded area. Shade-loving plants will look as good growing through stones as through any other mulch and in certain cases, a shingly effect may be the best possible approach. Ferns, particularly those species that relish dry but cool conditions will establish quickly. Hellebores seed rapidly in gravel and, provided a good selection of parent plants is introduced, the progeny will contain some useful hybrids. It is said that slugs dislike travelling over sharp grit and if this is so it makes sense to try surrounding some of the susceptible plants with a slug repellant cordon. Hostas are notorious for being disfigured in their youth, the resulting ugly holes remaining in the leaves all summer. Meconopsis can also suffer slug attack along with certain dicentras and most plants with soft, fleshy young shoots. Where drainage is especially important, the gravel can be dug in a little deeper than merely the top layer. I had the idea that the petiolarid primulas – particularly *P. whitei* might grow in shade for me if I planted them in a deep, peaty gravelly mix. But they died as quickly there as they did in my conventional shaded border. Clearly, gravel gardening in shade helps some but not all plants!

Summary

1. Flexibility is the key word. Planting schemes can run from strictly formal (knot gardens of box hedging in gravel) to complete *laissez-faire*

2. Herbs grow well in gravel

3. Gravel helps to enhance some shade-loving plants

4. Gravel makes a good mulch for raised beds or gardens

5. Plants especially amenable to gravel culture are marked in the Plant List

Maintenance

The object of this book is to help you to garden well in limited time. Using gravel will help you to achieve this result. Maintenance jobs vary according to the style of gravel gardening you adopt but in every case, routine tasks are made easier by the presence of the gravel.

Weeds

Prevention of seeding is all important. Mostly, in clean gardens, this can be done by hand pulling anything that shows. Perennial weeds, if they appear, may need the more drastic action described in Chapter One. Hairy bittercress, that garden centre scourge that can green over a clean surface before you can say 'William Robinson', is disastrous on gravel, needing to be hoed or pulled as soon as spotted. With the *laissez-faire* gravel garden in spring, when weed seedlings appear together with wanted self-sown plants, the choice of action is straightforward: either

Remove as many of the plants as you want to save in a given area, hoe or spray, then re-plant the saved seedlings, or:
Hand weed and thin the wanted seedlings at the same time.

Which of these options you take depends on how bad the weed infestation is. Usually, after the first couple of years, by which time the flora will have settled down, a quick run through once a month is enough.

With more formally planted scree, hoeing is easy enough but watch out for weeds hiding under sprawling plants like helianthemums. A single groundsel overlooked can seed and cause a nasty outbreak. With weeds, vigilance is the key. Get into the habit of pulling up everything you see *when* you see it. Never think: 'there's a sowthistle, I must pull that up next time I pass.' Do it now! A few seconds now will save future hours.

An important tip: gravel is hell to kneel on so a pair of knee pads is a worthwhile investment.

Planting

Whenever a gravel mulch is disturbed, soil shows round the moved area. When you have finished planting, and step back to admire your handiwork, you'll be saddened to see the view spoilt by streaks and lumps of soil. No matter how carefully you work, these stains are unavoidable. They are not a problem however, and will disappear after the first rain. Where planting is to take place, it helps first to scrape back some of the gravel to prevent it from falling into the hole you dig but there is no need to go to great lengths to put clean gravel back in position. It is self-cleaning. In shaded areas, a greenish layer of algae may form but, where this is considered unsightly, a light raking over will freshen things up.

Direct sowing seed is the simplest job of all. Just scatter it where you want the plants. Rake it in if this makes you feel more comfortable but whether you do or not, the seeds will find their own way to the moisture and come up just the same.

Lifting perennials to divide them can make quite a mess. It pays to scrape the stones back before you start and to carry whole plants away from the scree before you set to and split them.

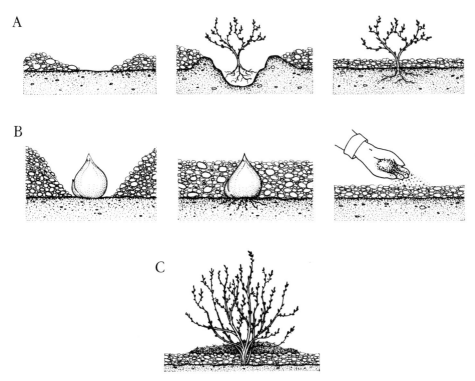

Fig. 9 Planting in gravel
A Scrape away gravel; plant the plant; return gravel
B Bulbs and seeds
C Climbers and shrubs (as with A but add mulch)

Feeding

Manure enthusiasts will be horrified by gravel. It is neither feasible nor desirable to top dress gravel gardens with any organic material at all. The humus content of soil under a gravel mulch could decline over the years but there is no reason to suppose that it will. There will always be root debris in the soil and some rotting plant material is bound to filter through from the top. The process of rotting takes place very near the surface in any case and will not proceed deep in the soil. The traditional herbaceous border or bedding scheme always depended on heavy feeding for a good display. In gravel gardens, the idea of lush, over-fed perennials doesn't fit. Thus, heavy feeding is not recommended. However, an annual dressing of general fertiliser is beneficial. Growmore or agricultural spring cereal fertilizer - about 20 per cent nitrogen with 10 per cent each of phosphorus and potassium – can be scattered at an average rate of $\frac{1}{2}$ oz (14.1 g) to 1 oz (28.3 g) per 1 sq yd (0.8 sq m). No more! If, when I scatter this in March, I notice something hungry like a rose or a fast-growing perennial, I put a little extra near its roots. However, the whole approach is very haphazard and I only go on spreading as long as my arm doesn't ache too much. Organic gardeners who dislike artificial fertilisers can use blood, fish or bone meal in the same way – but watch your hygiene!

Climbing plants, particularly clematis, are extremely hungry and love smelly mulches. For them and them alone I am prepared to break the rules and pile a little compost over their roots. One can scrape back the gravel for this but I seldom bother. The lower leaves and surrounding plants soon cover the eyesores. Occasionally, especially after a hateful cold spring, I wander about with a can full of liquid manure – usually diluted to half the manufacturer's recommended strength – giving a pint or two to what I regard as being deserving cases. This is especially helpful to new additions.

The ability of plants to absorb nutrients through their leaves must not be overlooked. Foliar feed can impart a uniquely healthy glow to almost everything – something to ease the worries of those who feel their gravel plants are missing out because they are not getting their yearly treat of horse muck. It is worth remembering that foliar feeds sprayed in strong direct sunlight, especially in a hot, dry garden, can result in leaf-burn so spraying in the early morning or late evening is less risky. Seaweed-based organic foliar feeds are more gentle.

Water

One of the big disadvantages of any mulch is that it disguises the state of the soil beneath. Although pea gravel helps to keep soil cool and moist, eventually, in a low rainfall area, it can dry out. The problem is that signs on the surface are that all is well. Clearly, if there has been no rain for some time, it will pay to to scrape back some gravel and have a look. Alternatively, if you notice drought stress among the plants, they probably need water. Midday wilting, yellowing of silver foliage, cessation of growth are the more obvious signs. The most common problem associated with watering is that few people provide enough. The 'little and often' rule is not one to be obeyed. A sprinkle on the surface every other day for two months will do no good at all. If you have a rain gauge, setting this up within range of sprinkler can be very revealing. A good ½ in (12 mm) of rain equivalent will be needed. Irrigation at night is best because the water has more time to soak in before evaporation takes place. Thus, if you use a simple hose-fed irrigator, relying on mains water pressure, leave it running in the same place for at least an hour. This is true for the whole garden and will, even if you are metered for water, make more efficient use of it than a series of short sprinkles.

The autumn clean-up

As things die down for the winter, more of the gravel becomes visible. The great temptation is to chop everything back before Christmas and go into winter with the whole garden shipshape, Bristol fashion or whatever. But there are strong arguments for leaving much of the cutting back until spring. On gravel, especially where tender plants are to be over-wintered, cutting back should be left until March in warm areas and April wherever heavy, sustained frost is likely after the spring equinox. A quick whip through, removing dead or broken branches but leaving as many of the plants as possible alone will pay dividends in the spring. At the same time, you want to enjoy your gravel all through the year so, to avoid a complete mess, anything that is really unsightly can be removed. Bulbs will begin to flower in late January in a mild year so clearly, it is pointless to grow them if they are to be spoilt by being covered with last year's dead perennials. It's a matter of judgement but, the more you cut back in autumn, the greater the risk of winter damage.

Summary

1. Control weeds by preventing seeding

2. Work over gravel areas monthly, hand pulling annual weeds and treating perennial weeds with glyphosate

3. Plant straight into gravel, scraping back the surface first

4. Feed once a year with up to 1 oz (28.3 g) Growmore or equivalent per 1 sq yd (0.8 sq m).

5. Look out for signs of drought stress. Water thoroughly when it occurs

6. When cleaning up in autumn, avoid cutting dubiously hardy perennials such as penstemons back. Leave them entire until spring

CHAPTER FOUR

The Wild Garden

Like it or not, every garden contains uninvited guests. Some are welcome: the first swallows, the spring arrival of robins in North America or stray primroses in Devon. Others are less popular: slugs, greenfly, thistles or rodents. The purpose of this chapter is to show how we can take maximum advantage of these gifts from nature and at the same time, tone down some of her more destructive elements.

Wildlife is an essential ingredient of all good gardens. Without it they are sterile and artificial. But with extremism in almost every walk of life these days, it is not surprising that certain crusading ecologists have been exhorting gardeners to give their land to the wilderness. Only wild flowers should be grown, they say, telling us to plant none but ecologically useful trees like willows, hawthorn and oak. Our lawns should not be close mown but instead, should become fertile meadows, full of native grasses and flowers. The only roses we should grow are wild briars which must be allowed to form impenetrable thickets where linnets can nest and winter migrant birds feed on the hips. This is buncombe! The most ardent naturalist can develop broad habitats for a wealth of wild species without compromising the quality of the garden in any sense at all. Indeed, by providing certain features for the benefit of the wildlife environment, your garden will be greatly improved.

There is another dimension: wildlife and the *laissez-faire* technique go hand-in-hand. Liberal gardening practices work in harmony with nature, meaning that uninvited guests can benefit as much as the plants you have nurtured. Encouraging wildlife in the garden is worthwhile because it:

Adds another interest
Provides an extra source of beauty
Is educational for children and adults
Improves our understanding of environmental issues
Can break the ice at parties

Adding interest to a garden is always worthwhile. There are those who prefer not to have creepy-crawlies lurking in the shrubberies and one must respect their feelings. However, few people, especially if they are fond of plants and gardening, can fail to be fascinated by some of nature's more bizarre features. Watching an exhausted willow warbler bringing up a baby cuckoo three times its size, for example or even studying the hierarchy of an ant colony.

Extra beauty comes in all shapes and sizes. Wildflowers often make first-rate garden plants, keeping the more exotic subjects company without becoming a nuisance. No matter how skilfully contrived, a mixed border can seldom match up to the joy of a woodland ride in May – a haze of bluebells and pink campion in Europe; a dazzling sea of wake robin with erythroniums, columbines and smilacina in North America – but using natives helps to capture some of the magic. Visiting birds and insects can be as rich a source of beauty as anything grown: imagine a blowsy purple buddleia surrounded by a cloud of greedy butterflies, or being lucky enough to live in a part of the world where humming birds hover like gems among late jasmine blossoms. The joy of watching a kingfisher by the garden pond is worth a dozen replacement goldfish!

The educational aspects are self-evident. For children, a thousand words in school biology books cannot compete with the experience of following the life cycle of a frog from spawn to froglet or of a butterfly from egg to adult. Plant taxonomy is simpler to puzzle out with wild species than with cultivars, particularly if they are growing within a step or two of the back door. Relationships between species in the habitat can be observed at close quarters – there's a lot to be said for bird watching through the living-room window, particularly in cold weather when you can have your bottom in a strategically positioned chair, a fire crackling in the grate, one hand on your field glasses and the other firmly round the whisky tumbler.

Breaking the ice at parties is a semi-facetious heading. Thankfully, more and more people are becoming aware of the plight of so much of our wildlife. It is fashionable, these days, to discuss such matters and those who don't care or don't know about ecology often become converted when they see nature in action at close quarters. At a barbecue recently, our guests were startled but delighted to see a kestrel swoop into a border near where they were standing and take off with a small field vole. The bird was so close they could see its markings quite clearly.

Having touched on some reasons for fostering wildlife, the next step is to see how this fits in with our *laissez faire* method. Wildlife and liberal gardening go together comfortably but there are pitfalls to avoid and, as with everything else in life, there's an easy and a hard way. Rather than allowing a general free-for-all, many people prefer to set aside a specific area for wildness.

Setting aside a 'wild' area

For our purposes, the term 'Wild Garden' means an area devoted to wild plants. It may not be exclusively for natives but they will predominate the planting. The most popular site for such gardens is under trees. Often these are in old orchards or, lucky for some, where remnants of woodland have been preserved. The most effective I have ever seen was in Western Australia where, a few miles outside Perth, some new houses had been built on a particularly rich piece of bush. 'How d'ya like the yard?' I was asked. ('Yard' is the Australian for garden – even Wisley is a series of 'yards'.) Looking round I could see wild orchids, kangaroo paw, helichrysums and a host of other

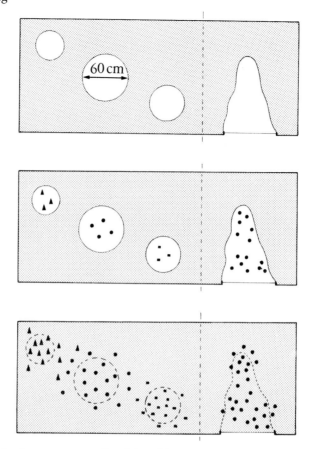

Fig. 10 Planting in grass: spray off, or lift turf from, area (year 1); plant and after-care (year 2); final result (year 3)

colourful treasures interspersed with reddish boulders and scrubby bushes. It was impressive. 'We just burn 'er off every few years, to stop the scrub getting too thick'. Few of us are that lucky. Gertrude Jekyll had woodland to work on and produced superb results; many Cornish gardens consist mainly of camellias and rhododendrons among which native flowers and grasses are allowed to flourish. But even a new building site with little more than tortured subsoil can be converted to a wild garden. All you need is time and patience.

A site under deciduous trees offers two main advantages: herbaceous species which enjoy shade often flower in spring and early summer, before the leaf cover overhead becomes too dense. Thus, the best part of the show takes place when the area is lightest. Secondly, grasses grow less vigorously in shade. Grass is the biggest problem with almost all wild gardens. It is so dominant in well-lit areas that often, even the most vigorous flowers are starved out of existence. And yet, some grass may be essential for keeping out rampant perennials such as stinging nettles. One has to strike a balance.

Establishing a wild garden from scratch

This will present more of a challenge than any other project in the garden. Patience is the key, rather than hard work. If you have no shade at all, you must begin by planting one or two trees. For small gardens, large, forest species are quite unsuitable. Smaller trees are often more decorative but still serve a useful function. Mountain ash or rowan, for example, has cream blossoms and good red berries which will feed winter migrants. There are some improved forms which will make better garden plants than the wild rowans without sacrificing any ecological merit. Hawthorn (*Crataegus sp.*) grows into a well-shaped tree and garden forms are as ecologically desirable as wild species, provided single flowered varieties are grown. Double flowers tend to be sterile and therefore fruitless for winter birds. Willows are often too large and weeping willows a ghastly mistake – they take up far too much room and offer little in return. Field maples (*Acer campestre*) stay reasonably small, having vivid autumn coloration

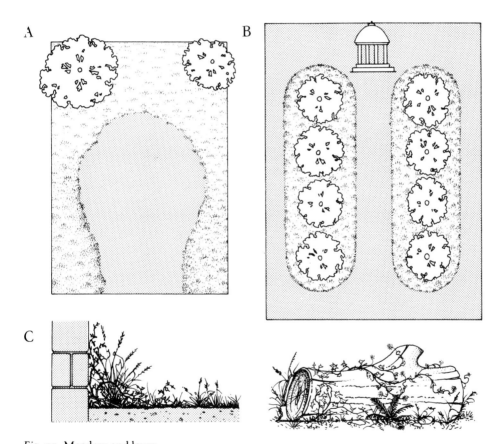

Fig. 11 Meadow and lawn
A Mixture of close-mown lawn and long margins
B Avenues: areas left long, perimeters cut short
C Other cover: base wall, fallen tree trunk

and wild cherry gives a good spring display as well as feeding birds. Planting wild trees is by no means essential. Fruit trees, particularly apples, will give shade, spring beauty and the bonus of a crop. Surplus or damaged fruit are valuable to a number of wild species such as late butterflies as well as birds. Evergreens give winter shelter and make good nesting sites.

Having established the trees, preparing the ground can be along similar lines to those described in Chapter Two for mixed borders. Eliminating any invasive perennial weeds is as important here because, if allowed to remain, they will smother everything else, even wild plants. A mix of grass seeds can be sown – preferably a mix made up of native grasses without ryegrass.

Plant establishment

There are two choices: either to sow wild seeds directly with the grass or to transplant. If seeds are sown, the grass must be thin enough not to smother them but thick enough to inhibit undesirable colonisers like groundsel or sowthistles. With the recent surge in demand and lag in responding supply, there are some seed mixes of dubious quality on the market. Some mixes contain undesirable weeds and inferior cultivars rather than true wild stock. Furthermore, there is a tendency for such mixtures to be bulked up with too much seed of the rampant species like oxeye daisy and corn marigold and to contain too little choice material. Clearly, the best bet is to buy seed by the species rather than by the mix, or to collect your own. Even if you decide to grow from seed, it is best to sow it in trays or in a small nursery area so that young plants can be transferred when they are big enough to establish themselves. Spring-sown seed treated this way, would be ready for transplanting in autumn.

My own experience is that I have always managed better with plants. Just how they are planted depends on the site. In bare soil they can go in at the same time as the grass seed but should be grouped informally so that they can be cared for in their infancy. While they become established, it is crucial to reduce the grass competition. Before planting in existing grassland, it is necessary to remove roundels of turf, or to spray off patches about 2 ft (60 cm) in diameter with glyphosate. The wild plants are grouped in these roundels and kept weed free for at least a year. Once established, the original plants will produce seed to spread their colonies. However hard you try, dominant species will tend to threaten the rest. The whole situation is artificial and may take years to settle down to a balanced flora. But settle it will, and at that stage, there will be surprise arrivals of other species from the wild.

Where there is already shade – perhaps under trees or in the shadow of a building, establishment of the wild garden is quicker and easier. Some of the species already growing there may be acceptable. If the ground is covered by rough grass or lawn, this can be planted with bulbs – directly into the turf – and with wild plants, making roundels as before. In dense shade, the grass will be thinner and plants can be inserted with minimal disturbance to the sward. Wood spurge, hellebores and cow parsley can become established this way, with cyclamen for spring and autumn and anemones, primroses, oxlips, lily of the valley or whatever you fancy. Do not forget the ferns – there are so many and in very deep shade they may be the only plants that thrive.

As the wild plants colonise the ground, you may find that the grass dies out in places. There is no harm in this, provided the resulting bare patches fill with desirable species. Annual weeds can be troublesome here, smothering neighbours and then dying off, leaving a bigger bare patch impregnated with their seed. The secret of success is to monitor the plant population, weeding out anything that looks threatening. This may sound laborious but need not be too demanding of your time. A quick inspection will be enough for you to assess what kind of balance exists. Any action needed should then be taken quickly before the problem gets worse. Events can overtake the unwary.

For example, under our massive lime tree there is a wild garden which looks pretty from September, when the autumn cyclamen flower, to the end of June when the cow parsley (Queen Anne's lace) has gone to seed. One year I noticed one plant of a strange grass. The seeds were purplish and barbed – not unattractive – so I let it stay. Next year there was a lot more of it. The following year it was everywhere. I identified it as sterile brome, a scourge of arable farms in the area. The grass is annual, thank heavens, so there was nothing for it but to cut the whole area hard back in late May, before seed was set. Problem solved – the few remaining seedlings were hand rogued and a sharp eye is kept for a recurrence of the nightmare.

Introducing new plants to a wild garden needs care and thought. If they look as though they might be too invasive, they must be eliminated or their spread contained before they grab control. Conversely, plants that take a year or two to settle down may need protecting from their neighbours.

Management

The easiest wild gardens to manage are those which peak in spring and run to seed before the middle of July. Management then is along the lines of old-fashioned farming when hay meadows were cut once in the summer and livestock then grazed on the aftermath. Cutting too early prevents the plants from seeding; cutting too late can result in a coarse sward of tangled grasses that defy destruction. In order to give the broad-leaved plants an unfair advantage over the grasses, it is important *never* to

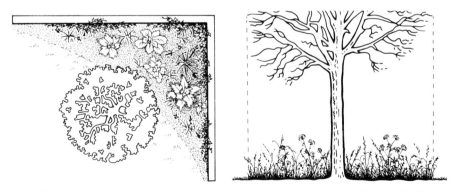

Fig. 12 Wild refuge: create a refuge in a garden corner or under a tree, within the drip-line

fertilise the area at all. (Unlike broad-leaved plants, grass has an almost unlimited response to nitrogen – the more it receives, the stronger it grows.) Because starving soil benefits the wildflowers, mown grass should be removed as often as possible. The optimum treatment is first to cut – you'll need a (mechanical) scythe, a lawnmower won't be up to such thick, high growth – and then to allow the grass to dry, ensuring the release of the seeds. Then, rake it up for burning or leave it heaped in a corner to rot down.

In densely shaded or grassless sites, there is still likely to be a tall stand of plants going to seed and these are best cut back in midsummer to allow the ground to green up again ready for the autumn display. The principle is the same as before but to avoid seed spreading, cut the plants back before they mature.

Meadows

The foregoing has dwelt on establishment of a wild garden within your garden plot. Once you have established a healthy environment for native plants, interesting native animals – insects, birds, mammals – are more likely to appear. On a much larger scale, similar principles apply. Wild meadows of several acres can be enhanced and enriched by introducing different compatible species. Obviously, large-scale management will be more demanding but one can develop little by little, perhaps by introducing extra plants along a particular path or in a known wet area. As far a woodland is concerned, management is beyond the brief of this slim volume. Woodland gardening consists, mainly, of going along with the tide but taking care that such species as brambles or bracken don't become wreckers of everything else.

There is more on meadows later. (See Chapter Ten.)

Summary

1. Cash in on existing wild features – shaded areas under trees, woodland, etc.

2. Establishment from scratch takes time rather than hard work

3. Plant trees for shade where none exists

4. Eliminate undesirable perennial weeds and ensure that they don't return

5. Unless the site is very large, colonies establish more easily from transplants than from direct-sown seed

6. Obtain pure seed stocks, sowing by species rather than by mixture

7. Eliminate grass competition where broad-leaved plants are becoming established

8. *Never* fertilise a wild garden

Encouraging wildlife elsewhere

So far, we have dealt specifically with the establishment of a wild garden. However, there is no pressing need for every garden to have its wild area. Even well-manicured plots, if you dislike the informality of the natural garden, can go a long way towards establishing wildlife territory without spoiling the looks. It is also perfectly feasible to develop the whole of your garden as a wildlife preserve without changing it to an unmanaged wilderness. When encouraging woodland flora in shaded areas, for example, similar rules apply to North American species as to European. Thus, an interesting woodland garden could be carpeted with bluebells, fritillaries, martagon lilies, trilliums or columbines – all from different parts of the world, but all compatible with deciduous forest floor. There is nothing here to go against our native ecology.

To accommodate interesting species, certain basic features are needed. These are:

Water
Winter cover for birds and animals
Nesting sites
Food supplies
Refuge from predators

Water

Every living thing needs water. If you build a garden pond, within hours of filling it you will see birds bathing there. In a day or two, insect larvae will appear in the water and, left to its own devices, your pond would develop an ecology all of its own. With a little help and encouragement from you, this ecology will evolve more quickly. At the same time, water improves the aesthetics of every garden. Plants and structures can be reflected in it, providing an extra visual dimension. Water plants can be beautiful in their own right and you can watch fish for hours on end while the stresses and strains of modern living ease themselves out of your consciousness and float away. So, there is no clash of interest. Ponds, streams or lakes – according to your circumstances – are as good for the beasties as for the beauty of your garden.

No matter what the shape, an ecologically worthwhile pond must have at least one shallow end where amphibious fauna can walk in and out. If a careless hedgehog falls into the water, it can swim well enough but must have a sloping area where it can scramble out. As far as size is concerned, the larger and deeper the better. It is far easier to develop a healthy aquatic environment if there is a large volume of water. The deeper the pond, the less likely it is to go foul and stagnant and the more suitable it is for fish. If you want tadpoles, forget the fish – they all love to eat frogspawn and tadpoles. So do newts. In the confines of a garden pond, a gang of common newts can wipe out a young tadpole population in a very short time.

Various gardening books give helpful advice on how to install a thriving pond, so repetition here is probably unhelpful. As far as *laissez-faire* gardening is concerned, ponds are beneficial because, properly set out, they require minimum maintenance in return for maximum enjoyment. Water plants usually look after themselves, though

49

some of the more vigorous kinds need thinning once a year. Some of the world's loveliest wildflowers are the marginals. Many species of iris, water forgetmenots, kingcups, mimulus and flowering rush are all examples of wild plants fit for a garden pond. I like to use watermint, partly because of the delicious aroma and partly because it forms a useful mat of roots in which other marginals can sit. Planting directly into mud at the pond's margins is better than using a collection of submerged pots and baskets. One of the problems with butyl-lined ponds is that containerised plants can migrate about the slippery bottom, ending up in the wrong position. After a westerly gale, for instance, everything is crowded on the eastern shore.

If you haven't room for a real pond, a small tub or old kitchen sink dropped into the ground will enable birds to drink and a couple of choice aquatics to grow even though it will be too small for fish.

Winter cover

When people talk about wildlife refuges, they mean places where wild species can find safety. The cruel world abounds with predators, poisons, diseases and starvation. Climate is even more life-threatening. Man may take a decade to change the population map of a given species but a single harsh winter can complete the job in a tenth of the time. One aspect of the rape of the English countryside by intensive agriculture in the last twenty-five years has been the removal of hedges, copses, damp corners and areas of rough scrubland. In far too many areas, the resulting landscape is hostile to birds, animals and plants which are not adapted to open spaces. Imagine an old-fashioned hedge running from east to west. On the shady side, woodland plants like primroses and violets would have flourished, nocturnal animals might have sheltered from the heat of the sun – well, what passes for heat in England – and insects adapted specifically to cool, sheltered conditions could have lived and multiplied. On the south side, there might have been rockroses, wild thyme, field scabious and other sun-loving plants. Lizards would have darted among the short grasses, hunting for flies, adders might have basked in the warmth and, in spring, sulphur-yellow brimstone butterflies would cruise the length of such hedges, searching for the more sedentary, greenish white females sitting on the food plant – buckthorn. At the end of the hedge, a gate might have led into a wood, home of foxes, badgers, nightjars in summer and short-eared owls in winter. Thirty years ago, such places were to be found everywhere. Now, those that remain are so small and isolated that many species are unable to maintain their population sizes. Wild communities in such small sites, with a wasteland of intensive cropping keeping them apart, are threatened because they cannot spread to new territory. In short, their cover is blown – blown away.

If we want wildlife in our gardens we must provide *cover*. On a tiny scale, 'cover' could mean no more than leaving a fallen log to rot. A host of insects and other invertebrates will take refuge under it and in it. First under the bark, then, as that sloughs off and falls away, into the wood itself. Rodents or amphibians might hibernate underneath it. The myth of the salamander coming out of the fire may have originated from the ancients spotting hibernating salamanders crawling out of logs set to burn.

Cover may be larger. An old hollow tree – accommodation for owls, bats, starlings or hibernating butterflies. Thick encrustations of ivy are desirable, not only for the dense, warm cover they offer birds and insects but also because the late berries and nectar from the October flowers provide food. Long grass or corners left unmown provide cover; so do flat stones, arranged over hollows or on soft earth near ponds. Even chinks in an old stone wall give shelter. Last autumn, our tactless Labrador disturbed a pair of grass snakes which were snatching a last hour of October sun. They disappeared into the old limestone wall quick as a flash.

All the cover described so far is specifically for the benefit of wildlife. Although none of it detracts from the quality of your garden, at the same time, it doesn't do a lot for it! But it doesn't take much management either. Trying to be less than scrupulously tidy, not clearing up too much debris from sheltered spots where the mess doesn't show, leaving perennials unclipped until spring, not pruning shrubs or trimming ivy, not close mowing all the grass – these are all practices which neither add to nor subtract from your work load. However, such small measures will do much to improve your habitat.

Cover which benefits wildlife and also enhances the quality of your garden is not quite so straightforward but can be achieved with careful planning. Wind wreaks havoc in new or bare garden sites, so building barriers is essential. (The better the panoramic views, the stronger the winds!) Gardens open to the north and west are doubly exposed but a southerly gale can soon cut a swath through a carefully sited garden, even when it has hills or trees on three sides. Walls, though they make useful maintenance-free structures and support climbing plants, are not such effective windbreaks as hedges. Hedges slow down the wind, walls just cause it to eddy over their tops.

Planting a hedge can be expensive because so many plants are needed. However, the benefits will begin to be felt a couple of years after planting and by the time five years have passed, you'll wonder how you managed without it. Good ground preparation is essential and, when planting deciduous plants you must trim back at least 30 per cent of the height. Brutal though this sounds, it will result in thick vigorous growth. Plant as thickly as you can afford and dig a good deep trench, enriching the soil you put back with slow-release fertiliser like bone meal or with well-rotted manure.

Choice of hedging material is wide but using a plant species suited to your soil and climate is important. Of deciduous trees, many gardeners champion beech. However, on heavy soils, hornbeam will outperform beech and is no more troublesome to trim. One annual clip in mid-July is all the maintenance needed and 6 ft (1.8 m) the

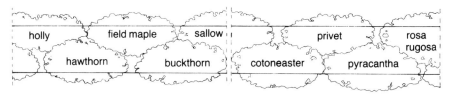

Fig. 13 Tapestry hedge (plan): wild hedge and exotic hedge

optimum height if the hedge is to be tapered to a thin top. I am tall and, having arms long enough to scratch my ankles without bending down, I am able to maintain my hornbeam hedge, just, at 7 ft (2.1 m). Shorter people should keep their hedges lower. It is an essential part of the *laissez-faire* method, not to have to climb a step ladder or mount a beer crate to clip the hedge. Such an exercise would double the length of time needed for the annual clip and that's not on!

The quickest evergreen for a formal hedge, though highly poisonous to livestock, is yew. Holly is much slower but makes a fine, dark background. For less formality, cherry laurel is a fast evergreen but has to be clipped with secateurs to avoid disfiguring the long leaves – hence, only a rough annual trim is possible in the *laissez-faire* garden. Plants like *Lonicera nitida* and privet, which need several clips a year, are best avoided. Informal hedges and screens can be composed from a mixture of shrubs which not only provide cover, slow down the wind and look attractive with flowers but also feed wildlife with their fruits. Several species of rose are useful, especially the fragrant *Rosa rugosa* whose huge hips are produced alongside late flowers, *Rosa moyesii* and its cultivars, and the low, scrubby burnet roses. Cotoneasters have a good range of berries as do berberis species, *Stranvaesia davidiana* and several good brambles. But all these plants need plenty of room and will be unruly. In more confined gardens, where hedges must be trimmed, there is still a wide choice of berrying species. Clipped pyracanthas often fruit well in hedges; so does *Cotoneaster lacteus* (silver reversed, green leaves and

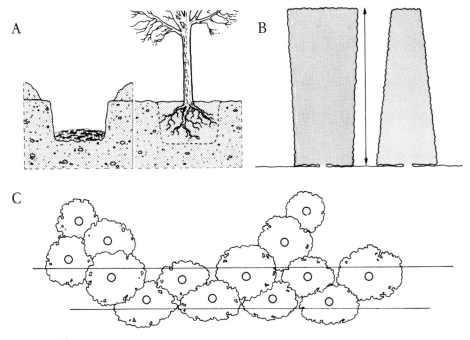

Fig. 14 A Planting
B Hedge shapes in section (*left,* wrong; *right,* ideal)
C Informal screen with bays (plan)

7. A seedling helianthemum which
   arrived in the author's gravel

8. Wall plants, like these *Erinus* will seed
themselves naturally once established.

9. A fine *Papaver somniferum*. Selected by
   weeding out inferior colours.

10. A colony of *laissez-faire* annuals:
    Cornflowers, *Salvia horminum* and
    Glaucium phoenicium

big clusters of red berries). In warm areas, escallonia is popular and flowers well. Even flowering currant, *Ribes sanguineum* makes a reasonable hedge with edible – to animals – fruits. 'Tapestry' hedges – composed of a series of different species – make a useful compromise and can look quite effective once established, though inevitably, the more vigorous plants tend to swamp the remainder. However, with wildlife in mind, they can be planted to provide permanent cover and a series of food sources from elder in September to snowberry in late winter.

Buildings and other garden structures make valuable cover. Outbuildings can be used as nesting sites by such birds as barn owls and as roosting areas for bats. Even new buildings can be designed to attract nesting birds. Installation of apertures into the roof cavity and building shelves for owl roosts may result in some interesting tenants! In the garden, features such as dovecotes and gazebos provide sites for birds and animals and, with a little extra thought, can be sited so that watching them is made easy.

Artificial nesting sites for birds are widely available these days – not just the traditional tit boxes but also such innovations as false martin's nests, made to look like mud and fixable on the average house's eaves. Siting is important as wrongly placed boxes can fail to attract customers. Furthermore, if natural sites abound, there is no need for artificial boxes. We have so many limestone walls that our tit boxes remained unoccupied for years while the bluetits nested all over the garden in the wall chinks. Eventually, field mice took over the boxes, multiplied and ate all my young clematis shoots.

Food supplies

Since the object of wildlife gardening in the *laissez-faire* style is to foster wild plants and animals without incurring too much extra work, the prospect of rushing about with pans full of scraps for the birds, bacon rind for the hedgehogs, biscuits for the badgers and fish pellets for the waterlife sounds far too much like hard work. Besides, regular feeding is, perhaps, at odds with the principle of conserving the *ecology*. If the environment is right, the food supply should be adequate for sustaining the resident species. Growing plants rich in food sources makes sense. Berry-bearing shrubs, and heavy seeders like sunflowers, are obviously helpful but so are plants with smaller seeds such as clematis, most members of the daisy family and a host of herbaceous perennials and annuals. The knack here is to avoid trimming back seeding plants unless they are likely to become an invasive nuisance. Food plants for butterflies come later but nectar feeds other insects besides lepidoptera.

Refuge from predators

Just as artificial feeding is dubiously beneficial, so, in a well balanced environment, is protection of species from predators. Clearly, nature should be allowed to take her course and anyway, hawks, foxes, stoats and weasels should be as welcome on your territory as their prey. After all, they are links in the food chain you are trying to forge. However, certain aspects of the garden are artificial: the garden pond, when there are

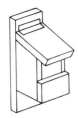

Fig. 15 Nesting boxes

herons about, becomes a deathtrap to its resident fish. Personally, I'd rather keep supplying the heron with fresh fish from the pet shop in return for the privilege of his company in my garden. Trout farmers are, understandably, less enthusiastic and if I had a collection of precious exotic fish, no doubt I'd be anxious to protect them with a wire mesh screen. It depends on your priorities. Frogs must be protected from newts while their colonies are building up. Other predators such as blackbirds and thrushes must be discouraged while the froglets are leaving the water.

The most troublesome domestic predators are cats, usually neighbours' cats, which patrol the garden regularly or swoop in for an occasional punitive raid. Artificial feeding of birds tends to improve the cats' chances of scoring hits but well-aimed water or lumps of soil – not half bricks! – discourage them from trespass without harming them. Pet repellents have never worked for me.

Summary

1. Ensure adequate water supplies. Ideally a pond, stream or lake – anything with sloping sides, the bigger and deeper the better

2. Improve the environment by ensuring plenty of *cover*:

   Hedges, trees or shrubs
   Leaving fallen branches, stones or slabs for things to live in or to hibernate under
   Some long grass
   Not cutting plants back until spring

3. Make sure there are plenty of nesting sites – not only in the planting areas but in or on buildings or garden structures

4. Keep a look out for excessive predation – especially by cats

Specific wildlife measures

Having looked at the general principles of wildlife establishment, a glance at some of the more specific treatments follows.

Wild flowers

First, let's define a weed: a weed is a plant growing in the wrong place – everyone knows that. Or do they? For years we've been trained to eliminate anything that hasn't been planted. Everything has tended to be compartmentalised – vegetables in the kitchen garden, alpines on the rockery and so on. In *laissez-faire* gardening there is no place for such strictures. We are growing what we like where we like. Wild plants from two sources will be growing in the *laissez-faire* garden – opportunists that have turned up and plants we have sought to introduce.

Not all opportunists are desirable. Bindweed, ground elder and couch grass are hated enemies but violets, primroses and salad burnet make welcome arrivals and marsh orchids, spurge laurel or musk mallow receive the red carpet treatment. Other species are welcome in one spot but anathema in others. Buttercups, white deadnettle, cow parsley, cuckoo flower, lesser celandine and white campion are all examples of plants of surpassing beauty. They are also invasive and difficult to control. Even in a wild garden, each of them can become too dominant for the balance of the planting. And yet, not only do they help to provide shelter for wildlife, they are also useful contributors in their own right. Thus, a sensible rule seems to be to let such plants grow in areas where they can be confined within boundaries and where they are not putting anything else at risk: rough corners, under trees, behind the garage or anywhere that will be richer for a green cover.

Several natives are gardenworthy enough to be planted on purpose. Many make good mixed border subjects and can join forces with exotic shrubs and perennials where they will enhance the natural look. Harebells, foxgloves, mulleins, bell flowers, rose campion, meadow cranesbill, cowslips, primroses, wood anemones, field scabious, great knapweed, wild arum and wood spurge are all examples of good mixed border plants. Wild shrubs such as guelder rose, daphnes, some of the dwarf willows and wild broom all blend in equally well, provided the rules regarding colours and textures are applied as much to them as to the cultivated plants. Again, it's a matter of taste. The botanical enthusiast with a yen for his country's natives is likely to have far more in the way of wild flowers in his garden than the lover of a more contrived set of artwork. Treatment and culture of such plants is much the same as with their domestic relatives and in many cases, improved forms of wild species are on the market – the dark leaved form of wood spurge, *Euphorbia amygdaloides* 'Rubra' for example, or golden leaved hazel. Gradually, as your garden develops over the years, a spread of both wild and cultivated plants will continue side-by-side until, hopefully, you no longer discriminate against any on grounds of race or origin but rather, on grounds of its habits and suitability within your scheme.

Butterflies and moths

Though they form a small fragment of the huge diversity of insect orders, butterflies are usually more welcome than anything else. The most unobservant individuals notice them and, since they neither sting nor bite, enjoy having them around. Of late, the press has been garrulous about butterflies, abounding with lists of nectar-rich flowers irresistible to them. Sadly, fostering the food plants, because they are usually so unglamorous, has received less coverage. Let us first define 'food plant': *A food plant is the plant on which the butterfly's or moth's larva feeds.* Each species will only breed on its own specific food plants. The larvae of peacock butterflies cannot feed on anything but stinging nettles. Small tortoiseshells are the same, though they can sometimes be induced to feed on hops in captivity. As luck would have it, these butterflies are strong flyers and, since nettles are common everywhere, it is not necessary to have them in the garden. There will still be plenty of visitations from both species, even if the nearest nettle patch is some distance away. The brown family *(Satyridae)* are much lazier, flitting about among long grasses. Holly blues, a species associated with old Victorian gardens rich in evergreens, are also quite local as are green hairstreaks, small coppers and skippers. Therefore, it seems sensible to plant the food plants of some of the insects. Here is a list of the more common British butterflies with their foodplants.

Butterfly	Food plant
Speckled Wood	Cocksfoot, couch
Hedge Brown Marbled White Meadow Brown Ringlet Wall Brown Small Heath	Many grasses
Most fritillaries	Violas
Peacock Red Admiral* Comma Small tortoiseshell	Common nettle
Painted Lady*	Thistle
White Admiral	Honeysuckle
Common Blue	Birdsfoot trefoil, rest harrow
Holly Blue	Holly, ivy
Small Copper	Sorrel
Green Hairstreak	Broom, rockrose
Orange Tip	Jack-by-the-hedge, Lady's smock
Brimstone	Buckthorn

* Red Admiral and Painted Lady are migrants.

Moths can be as interesting as butterflies. There are far too many to list but some of the hawk moths are impressive and food plants such as privet, willow, poplar and lime will attract them. Other species, such as puss moths – whose wonderful caterpillars are armed with whiplash tails – and red underwings feed on poplars. Many moths are attracted to the same nectar-bearing flowers as butterflies.

Attracting the adult insects is not difficult. Most species of Buddleia, particularly *B. davidii* are the most popular shrubs. Flowering time is easy to adjust with buddleia by pruning at different times. Bushes cut back hard in March will flower in July but May pruning – really vicious hacking, that is – will result in large crops of flowers in early autumn. One drowsy September afternoon I counted 13 small tortoiseshells on a single panicle. Other butterfly flowers for summer include *Sedum spectabile* and all its hybrids and cultivars, *Verbena bonariense* and the mildew resistant form of Michaelmas daisy, *Aster novi-angliae*. For early season, honesty, cuckoo flower and aubrieta are popular with over-wintered tortoiseshells as well as new season orange tips and whites. Lavender seems to appeal to all nectar feeding insects.

Other Insects

In the enthusiasm for butterflies it is easy to forget that other insects are not only interesting but essential for successful balance in the environment. They feed birds and some mammals; they pollinate plants and help in the processes of decay. Water will enable you to have dragonflies and other aquatic insects. Walls and banks are often homes for the various species of bee that will be working in the borders. Bees are host to various parasitic insects, not to mention a vast variety of natural mimics, evolved to resemble them for their own protection. The more you look at insects, the more fascinating they become. Perhaps there is a touch of Fabre in all of us!

Pests

Whether fully organic or chemical crazy, every gardener is troubled by pests. Plant diseases ruin his crops, insects munch his young plants or suck juice out of them – spreading deadly viruses – rodents gnaw, birds peck, moles dig up lawns and children ransack fruit trees. *Laissez-faire* gardening does not mean sitting back, allowing destruction to take its course. A sensible approach is needed to control pests and to weigh the odds in favour of the plants in the garden. Chemical control may or may not be used according to your creed. This does not have to go against the concept of wildlife conservation. Few flowering plants need prophylactic spraying. The chief exceptions are roses and even with these, the two main diseases – mildew and black spot – can be prevented with a small number of fungicide applications. (See Chapter Seven.) Even then, selecting disease resistant varieties goes a long way towards eliminating the need for chemical control.

Insects can be troublesome, but one can live with outbreaks unless they become severe. Aphids vary in the strength of their attacks from year to year. If they do begin to destroy plants, remember to spray only after the bees and other flying insects have retired. Alternatively, try a forcible hose of water – that can dislodge many of them without the need of chemicals. Perhaps the best house rule is to keep the sprayer in the shed except for dire emergencies. To be exclusively organic however, creates more work. Each of us has to decide whether we prefer the extra work or the chemical – which is the lesser evil.

Gnawing rodents and troublesome birds are more difficult to tackle. If you grow a number of bulbs and corms, voles or mice will create havoc from time to time. Traps can be effective, installed in drain pipes or under pots so birds can't get at them. Poisons are less desirable because scavengers eating the affected corpses can become poisoned themselves. However, there have been years when, in desperation, I have resorted to mouse bait. With birds, the problem is scaring the bad ones away without disturbing the beneficial species. Sparrows can be guarded against by spreading black cotton over target plants. Provided it is kept taut, there is no risk of their becoming entangled. Shooting with an airgun is one solution which the less squeamish and more bloodthirsy adopt, but the noise, even though they are much quieter than shotguns, seems to scare anything with wings out of its wits – rare migrants more than sparrows.

Summary

1. Site wild plants with care:

   Choice plants in mixed borders, gravel garden or rock garden
   Invasive, but beneficial plants within controllable boundaries
   rapacious weeds out!

2. Consider garden forms of wild plants. Some make excellent *laissez-faire* subjects

3. Remember butterfly and moth food plants as well as nectar rich flowers

4. Accommodate other insects, they are part of the cycle of nature, but:

5. Pest infestations have to be controlled, even in a nature-lover's *laissez-faire* garden

CHAPTER FIVE

Annuals and their Uses

Annuals do not add to the workload. In fact, in the *laissez-faire* garden they help to reduce it. Because they germinate, grow, flower and die as soon as their seed is set, they are often associated with heavy management – preparing the ground every spring or autumn, sowing, thinning, supporting, feeding and clearing out at the end of the season, ready for doing the whole thing all over again. The Victorian style of bedding out tender plants *en masse* to create dazzling carpets is still widely imitated, mostly in parks and corporation plantings but also in a good many private front gardens. Annuals are often used for these garish schemes and, because they give rise to such killing work, have earned themselves a bad reputation. This is unfair and we must clear our minds of any lingering prejudice. Annuals can contribute much to our gardens in return for very little effort.

Categories

Strictly speaking an annual is a plant that lives for no more than one season. However, because several other types of plant can be treated like annuals, we can cover four distinct categories in this chapter: hardy annuals; biennials; tender (or 'half hardy') annuals; tender perennials. But first, let us look at the advantages of each.

Advantages

In *laissez-faire* gardens, the first two categories are likely to be the most widely grown because they give the best results for the least work input. The aim is to take a little trouble in the early stages, to see that they have been introduced in the right places, but then to let them get on with replenishing their own stocks without much more effort on your part.

The strong points of annuals are:

They take up little space
They can add splashes of colour at the right times to heighten climax periods
They can occupy difficult spots

They make good follow-on plants from spring bulbs

They can fill gaps at short notice

Because of their ephemeral nature, annuals make a conspicuous show while they flower but, once over, they leave little mess behind. Early species flower and die, giving space for later plants. This enables you to increase the plant population of your mixed borders or gravel gardens without enlarging the area used for plants.

Every border has shortcomings and getting the balance to artistic perfection can take a long time. Gertrude Jekyll worked on her borders at Munstead Wood for about 40 years, constantly polishing and perfecting the planting. Annuals, as she very well knew, are a useful way to bulk up on certain colours quickly. The original wild species are usually – but by no means always – quite restrained in their appearance but florists' forms and modern hybrids have large, bright flowers. Though it is fashionable to eschew these in 'tasteful' modern gardens, we should bear them in mind when a particular chromatic explosion is needed. The joy of using annuals is that if they turn out to have been a ghastly mistake, nothing is lost. The plants will only last a few months and if they are too unbearable, even for that period, they can be pulled up without incurring huge losses.

Because of the opportunist nature of many annual species, they can occupy patches of ground that are too poor to sustain anything more substantial. Plants whose natural habitat is desert, for example, germinate in the wild immediately after rain, having a week or two to flower and seed before the water supply runs out. Several garden annuals behave in a similar fashion, producing continuous crops of flowers for as long as conditions permit. Often, all that is needed from the gardener is a little help in getting the parent stock plants established. From then on, they are happy to be fruitful and multiply unaided.

In any border where there are deaths, losses or changes of heart in the planting, gaps occur. Annuals make useful temporary fillers while more permanent planting becomes established, or to tide you over for the rest of the season. After bulbs, even where they are naturalised in grassland, certain annuals make a useful follow on during that dreary period when the bulbs have finished flowering but mustn't be cut back until the leaves have begun to wither. For some years, a thick planting of *Narcissus poeticus* in my garden was followed by field poppies, the whole area not being cut back until late July when they had set some seed. Annuals can make good ground-cover plants, provided they are reasonably permanent – a seeming self-contradiction but meaning that the young seedlings must become well-established as soon as the old parents are gone. Now for a look at each category to see how they fit in with our liberalised approach to gardening:

Hardy annuals

This will probably be the most interesting group because its uses are so diverse. Much of the cultural detail applies equally to other categories but hardy annuals, once started off, should need the least attention. These are plants which will survive and multiply by producing seed without any form of artificial protection, even in areas where there is a likelihood of frost for up to six months of the year. Cornflowers and field poppies are European examples; clarkia and limnanthes behave the same way in North America.

Not everything about hardy annuals is good. There are several undesirable features which can cause problems. Invasiveness is particularly bad in certain species. In poor growing conditions this feature becomes an advantage but in mixed borders, particularly on rich soil, invading annuals can be ruinous. Genera such as Papaver, Salvia, Limnanthes, Calendula, Delphinium, Echium, most grasses, Senecio and Viola need careful watching. They all have invasive species but are far too good to expel altogether. The approach varies according to where they are grown but the same principles apply to all: where proliferation is to be limited, try to prevent too much seed from spreading. Poppies are heaviest seeders. Each pepper-pot capsule seems to contain thousands of seeds and when these fall unchecked, the ground all round a single plant can green over completely in a few days. Hoe these out and the next shower of rain will stimulate a second germination. Eliminate that and the following spring the ground will be almost as thick with seedlings again. Thus, most plants should be removed before they seed. With the larger poppies, a few specimens will provide plenty of colour so weeding most of them out as soon as the last flower has dropped its petals will not be too time consuming. With smaller species – field poppies, Shirley poppies and *Eschscholtzia californicum* – too much weeding out would be laborious, particularly where large colonies are grown. These species are therefore probably more suitable for planting in self-perpetuating colonies. Even then, a certain amount of policing is needed. With all annuals in borders or gravel, a limited amount of thinning will result in better, longer-lived plants that make a more positive statement. Six well grown cornflowers are more desirable than 30 weedy individuals all fighting for room.

Establishment – first year

Getting hardy annuals to carpet whole areas or to colonise difficult corners needs a different approach from filling border gaps. However, the initial task of plant establishment is much the same. The seed can be sown direct or transplanted. Most seed packets instruct you to sow where the plants are to flower and to thin out when they have emerged. But this may not be the easiest way. If we want to establish a healthy colony quickly, it may be useful to raise stock plants in trays and transplant them when they are growing vigorously.

When planting out in mixed borders, don't fall into the trap of making artificial looking groups and don't plant in threes! The idea is to fill the gaps but to create the impression that nature has done the job, not you. By all means place groups in single areas but you should disperse other plants and small fragmentary clumps in amongst the existing vegetation, thus composing the picture. When planting for difficult corners, direct sowing may result in failure but transplanting could produce just enough robust plants to saturate the ground with seed and therefore start a community. Stony sites or barren yard corners are a particular challenge but there is at least one species that will survive in such hostile terrain. Plant thickly but don't despair if there are heavy losses in the first year. For ground cover, direct sowing may work as quickly because the species you use are likely to be small, rapid growers which defy destruction and seed everywhere.

Subsequent years

After the first season, your problem will not be too few, but too many offspring. In a well-balanced border, competition from the rest of the flora will help to control the annuals – up to a point. As with other aspects of *laissez-faire* it's a matter of policing and intervening when necessary, before a minor imbalance develops into a crisis. There may even be a need to restrict the perennials in places to allow the annuals a little living space. Where self-sown plants are sparser than you would like, lift healthy specimens from other spots to bulk up. Usually, there is no shortage of plants, merely a less than perfect distribution. Such minor adjustments can be completed in a very short time as part of general spring maintenance work.

Summary

1. Grow varieties that will develop self-perpetuating colonies

2. Consider raising plants in trays and transplanting in the first year to establish good, vigorous parent stock

3. Be careful about siting invasive annuals in mixed planting

4. Take extra care to establish first plantings in difficult corners

5. Aim for a limited number of well-grown specimens rather than a thickly sown mass

6. Select for colour and habit by weeding out undesirables before they set seed and preferably as soon as their first flowers are visible

7. Keep an eye open for new varieties which might be worth introducing. You won't know which ones will suit your soil and multiply well for you until you have tried them

---

Biennials

Plants that grow vegetatively one year and flower the next before dying have different needs from the annuals. Some are as attractive in their vegetative stages as in flower. Much of the advice for hardy annuals goes for biennials also.

Tender annuals

The term 'half-hardy', though it has been used for donkey's years, is ridiculous. A plant is either hardy or tender – it depends on the plant and on where it is grown. Wallflowers are hardy in England but tender in New England, for example. *Nicotiana sylvestris* is hardy in Madeira but tender in Scotland. For our purposes, we can assume 'tender' to refer to any plant that will not survive unprotected in a garden that has sustained frost in winter.

Though associated with bedding, and therefore anathema to the *laissez-faire* gardener, there are several good uses for certain tender annuals. Even a zero labour garden will look better for a container or two planted up on its terrace. Instant colour in otherwise dull borders can be arranged, at a price, by planting groups of tender annuals some of which are far too beautiful to lose in a sea of bedding. Disgusting though they look massed with red salvias, African and French marigolds must not be dismissed out of pure snobbery. They flower for a long time; they come in a useful range of colours, from lemon to dark tan, and they are very undemanding. Extra feeding is necessary for optimum results but the reward is a whole season of trouble-free flowering. To many people, the smell is pleasant too – a sort of tropical resonance to it somehow – and, at the end of summer, they are so easy to pull up. There are other plants of equal merit, depending on your taste, which help to enrich summer plantings. It is not always very artistic to use bright bold colours but in summer sunlight colour intensity is reduced so, provided there are plenty of relieving green areas for the eye to roll over, a spot of razzle dazzle is not nearly as frightful as the greenery yallery brigade would have you believe. The problem arises when one is confronted by indiscriminate, hedge-to-hedge kaleidoscopes with about as much appeal as a 'technicolor yawn'. To those one can only say, Ugh!

Tender annual plants are costly but, because you are not investing in a whole bedding scheme, the outlay need not run to unrealistic figures. With a heated greenhouse or even a windowsill propagator, they can be raised from seed but this will involve heating costs and more fiddly work. For small quantities, growing from seed may prove to be a false economy but the choice of plants is usually wider. If you want a particular variety, seed may be your only source. Incidentally, few tender annuals thrive in shade. The best temporary plants for dark areas are probably impatiens (busy lizzies) which have been bred to produce almost every colour except blue or yellow.

Tender perennials

In warm countries, these would go on for ever but, because of the nature of Britain's northern climate, we tend to treat them as annuals, raising new plants every year, either from seed or from cuttings. Well-known summer flowers like pelargoniums (usually, wrongly, called geraniums) fall into this category but there are hundreds of less familiar plants which can be useful in summer without piling on too much work.

Reproducing such plants is not difficult but over-wintering them can be trouble-some. Some are so attractive, however, that it seems to be worth the extra trouble to

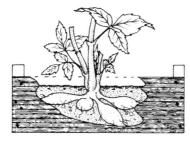
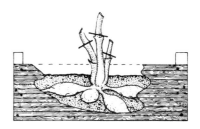

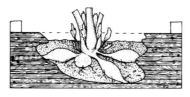
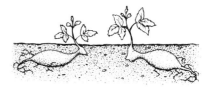

Fig. 16 Overwintering tender plants
October: lift or pot into deep trays (peaty compost), trim lightly (cool greenhouse, moist but not wet)
March: cut back hard
April: shoots emerge – cutting taken or divisions made
Late May: plant out

keep them. Furthermore, their level of hardiness is variable. In some areas, certain sub-tropical plants will cruise happily through all but the fiercest of winters whereas further south they may die with scarcely a frost. Temperature alone, it seems, is not to blame. Survival depends on how closely the plant is suited to your environment. Rain, snow, sunshine, temperature fluctuation, wind, soil type and latitude all interrelate to produce a unique combination of factors in every garden and the only way to find out exactly what will survive in yours is to plant it and see. Obviously, the extreme cases can be ruled out. No one would bother to plant frangipani or bougainvilleas outdoors in England just as a Maltese gardener would have a miserable time trying to get petiolarid primulas to survive. However, allegedly tender subjects like the Mexican *Salvia patens* and *Viburnum odoratissimum*, a Malayan native, have survived air temperatures of −16°C in my Lincolnshire garden.

Tender perennials, because they come from sunny climates, are often brightly coloured and thus lighten the midsummer effect. Several flower late into the autumn to provide a welcome tropical feel. Some make useful container plants, others plug late gaps in borders left by early flowering perennials such as oriental poppies. As well as garden highlights, many of the tender perennials make useful background material for mixed plantings. Silver foliaged artemisias, helichrysums, variegated abutilons, scented leaved pelargonium species as well as the more showy types; even fuchsias have their place. Some of the shrubby salvias can be treated in precisely the same way as fuchsias but are far more interesting and several have the added bonus of aromatic foliage. *Salvia rutilans*, for example, smells exactly like pineapple.

Propagation is not difficult. Most produce viable seed which can be grown under glass but taking cuttings is easier. If you have a greenhouse, it is good policy to have a few rooted cuttings in stock all the time so that these can be brought out at any stage from May to August to use as emergency stopgaps. Cuttings can be taken at any time, as long as there is actively growing material on the plants. Rooting is usually trouble free, particularly if you have a propagator. (See Chapter Two.) Young plants, however, are more prone to winter kill than their parents so the earlier the cuttings are taken, the better their chances of survival.

Tender perennials must be considered because they come easily from cuttings and:

Provide showy flowers to highlight the season
Frequently flower on into autumn
Give a 'tropical' feel to an area
Make excellent container subjects

Laissez-faire plantings

Because of the time factor, most of the annuals we use must be self-perpetuating. There is time for a little gap filling with tender plants to highlight the colour of summer but, in the main, we need self-starters. In mixed borders, where pastel shades belong, honesty and foxgloves always go well. These can be supported by other tall flowering plants like rose campion *(Lychnis coronaria)* which has a silvery-white form, sweet rocket *(Hesperis matronalis)* and possibly even some of the paler evening primroses. In the border front, lower plants like nigella or candytuft colonise easily and *Salvia horminum* – often call clary – has coloured bracts which last all summer. There are pink, white and blue forms. In dry, bright conditions cornflowers and larkspurs can be used, either in mixtures, or in single colours. The true, wild cornflower is easily the best blue and, though more straggly in its habits, than 'improved' garden varieties, makes a delightful garden plant. If you can find seed for them, pure white larkspurs look outstanding planted among shrubs with dark foliage. Where they are growing to maximum potential, most of these annuals will benefit from the feeding regime of the mixed border.

The fronts of sunny borders make perfect sites for *Limnanthes douglasii*, named after the nineteenth-century plant hunter David Douglas – antithesis of the lofty Douglas fir. Limnanthes makes such a dense cover that even dandelions are smothered. The leaves are bright emerald green and emerge in autumn. By early spring, the first of a succession of vivid yellow blooms appear, each surrounded by a white rim so that one is reminded of a diminutive poached egg. Soon, the green disappears beneath a total cover of these bright flowers. I remember seeing a pure yellow form, without the white rims at Kew, but have been unable to find it in commerce – a pity because I preferred it. Limnanthes seeds furiously everywhere, and seems not to care what kind of soil it inhabits. In spite of this apparent invasiveness, it is not difficult to eliminate by hoeing if it becomes *planta non grata*.

In nooks, corners, paving cracks and so on, any annual is desirable that will not only tolerate the poor conditions but will thrive and multiply. The white form of moth mullein – not white at all really but pale beige with a violet eye – seeded itself in some old brick paving for me and very welcome it was too, even though the plants were unable to attain more than about half their normal height. Nasturtiums, horrid in most borders might transform a dreary expanse of car park and will grow on soilless rubble. Colonising shade is more difficult but there are plenty of perennials for that.

Collecting seed

The closing section of this chapter covers seed techniques and is relevant to other plants as well as annuals. However, since information on seeds and seeding has to go somewhere and, since annuals can only reproduce by seed, this seems as good a point as any.

Although in the *laissez-faire* garden, we will not expect to have to re-sow our annuals every year, nevertheless, on various occasions it makes sense to collect seed. Collecting seed is good practice because:

It is a way of safeguarding your collection
It ensures a plentiful supply of young plants
It provides material to give away or exchange
It provides the cheapest possible source of seed
It makes you more familiar with the characteristics of your plants

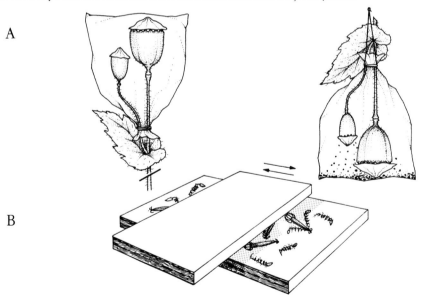

A

B

Fig. 17 Seed collection
A Paper bag over seed capsule; cut when first capsule ripens and hang it upside-down in a dry place until seed has shed
B Geranium: remove seeds by rubbing between two pieces of wood

A couple of important points:

1. F1 hybrids do not come true from seed. Therefore, offspring of F1 hybrids may well be inferior to their parents
2. It is not possible to reproduce a clone from seed

Harvesting

The golden rule is to collect before the seed is shed. This sounds silly but it is so easy to miss the bus. A ripening capsule checked regularly will hold onto its crop until, after a day's inattention from you, it will be discovered infuriatingly empty. Fixing paper bags over the flowering stems help to circumvent this problem but doesn't exactly work wonders for the appearance of your borders. Most veteran seed collectors have an empty envelope or two on them at all times so that a ripening capsule can be plucked. There are different techniques for different plants and too little space here to describe them all. However, some species are especially awkward. *Geranium* can be reluctant to yield up their seed when you try to take it, but explode their spring-loaded seed catapults on their own with the greatest of ease. Picking a full branch and, after drying it upside down in a paper bag, rubbing it between two flat pieces of wood can do the trick. Primulas are easily missed. Watch for the first capsule to open – a little star-shaped hole appears at the top end – and when it has, pick the whole flower stem and put it, head first into a paper bag. After a day or two, all the capsules will open, spilling their seed into the bag.

Hairy seed like clematis, pasque flowers and geums should be plucked gently from the receptacle. If the seeds come away easily, the capsule is ripe. Some people go to great lengths to snip off or rub off the hairy bits but I have found that they germinate just as well with them on, even when the seed pan looks most unprofessional with whiskers sticking up all over the place. Salvias produce seed in groups of four all the way up the stem. If you are short of stock plants and want to get maximum production, take the lower capsules first and work your way up the stem taking new seed every few days as it ripens. Berries can be disgusting – I once forgot that I'd filled a pocket with very ripe rose hips which gradually liquified and grew mouldy. Very uncomfortable, mouldy hips!

Storage

Once collected, the best thing to do with the seed is to sow it. The fresher the better. However, this is not always convenient and in certain cases sowing is better deferred until autumn or the following spring. Exceptions are most tree seeds. These must be sown fresh even though they then take a year or so to germinate. I try to sow paeony seed fresh too, but patience is the key word. In its first year it will produce a tiny root. The effort of doing that will prove almost too much for it and the shoot will not emerge until the second year. Thus, *Paeonia obovata* for example, should flower from seed within five years of sowing – if you're lucky. As well as sowing early, the second rule with woody plants is to hang on to the seed pans or keep the ground where they are sown carefully marked, so you know what they are. Do not give up – even after three years. They could still come!

Other seeds, particularly annuals, may be viable for years. They need to be stored cool and dry, and to be clearly labelled. After a lapse of some months, the words 'Cyc hed Elsa gdlf' may not jog your memory enough to remind you that the seed is *Cyclamen hederifolium* taken from your friend Elsa's garden because the leaf form was so much better than those in your own! Garden sheds and potting sheds are favourite places for seed storage but do make sure they are mouse free. Seeds are natural rodent food! Alternatively, store *dry* seeds in biscuit tins or rodent-proof boxes.

If the seeds are for your own use, it is unnecessary to clean them thoroughly. As long as the material is bone dry, a few leaf and seedcase fragments will do no harm at all. However, for most gardeners, seed becomes a currency for acquiring new strains and species from like-minded souls, in which case, cleaning is necessary. If you enter an official seed exchange scheme with a society (such as The Hardy Plant Society) cleanliness becomes essential. Most seed is easily cleaned by shaking it onto a large sheet of paper, then, with paper knife or ruler and gentle blowing, the dross can be separated from the gold. Excessively fine seed is tricky because it's so easy to blow away. One sneeze and a year's supply may be all over the potting shed floor! Large seed presents no such problem. All seed samples can be sieved to remove the larger pieces of debris – a flour sifter for fine seed, a coarser screen for big seed.

Having cleaned your sample, if you intend to distribute packets, you'll need small envelopes. I use $2\frac{1}{4}$ in (5.7 cm) square translucent Glassine inner envelopes – inserted into wages envelopes. A salt spoon or a home-made measure – try trimming down a cheap pen top – will enable you to produce equal sized portions. The amount in each portion is up to you but obviously, the finer the seed, the smaller the volume per hundred seeds!

Correct labelling is sensible practice for your own purposes and vital if you are distributing seed. Information on the packet must include the plant name. Also origin, date or year of collection, variety name (remember, you can't grow *clonal* varieties from seed) and any other brief, relevant information might help. Your seed packet should look like this:

> *Aster capensis* 'Santa Anita'
> Collected Careby Manor 7/88
> Original plant from Sissinghurst
> Note: (No other *A. capensis* at Careby, so should be pure)

If you type your label you will have reached the pinnacle of professionalism!

Seed from other sources may not, alas, be as reliable as your own. Many genera fail to breed true, especially when their seed has been collected in gardens where several different species of the same genus grow. Typical examples of dirty stock doing the rounds of many seed exchanging societies are aquilegias, violas, origanums and primulas. The chances of obtaining pure stock of such plants are remote unless they have been grown in isolation.

11. Wall top furnished with *Cheiranthus* 'Moonlight'.

12. A red-leaved form of wild woodspurge,
    Euphorbia amygdaloides 'Rubra'
    growing with the Turkish native
    Omphalodes cappadocica.

13. Ox-eye daisies (*Chrysanthemum leucanthemum*) and red campion (*Silene dioica*) used as cottage garden plants

14. Red admiral (*Vanessa atalanta*) on
    Aster novi-angliae.

Summary

1. Collect as soon as the first capsules ripen. Be careful not to miss the bus!

2. Label specimens clearly as soon as you collect them

3. Store in a rodent-free place, cool and dry

4. Clean seed if you intend to distribute it

5. Ensure adequate information on the packet

6. Watch for purity

Sowing

Different seed needs different treatment. All European primulas for example, can be autumn sown, in an unheated, uncovered frame so that they are exposed to maximum frost, snow and whatever else the winter decides to throw at them. Come spring, they will germinate like cress. Thus, the detailed instructions about putting them in the fridge, deep freeze, transferring them from the fridge to hot bench and so on is quite unnecessary. All that is needed is to make sure they receive some protection from severe frost in spring, *after* they have germinated. Even then, I've managed to raise good quantities of cowslips, auriculas and so on after sharp April frosts when I failed to cover the frames at night. Normally, closing the frame in the evening and opening it in the early morning will suffice but be sure to leave it fully open throughout January and February for vernalisation. (Vernalisation is the change in the nature of the seed which enables it to germinate after being exposed to periods of cold. This is a natural safeguard which prevents delicate seedlings from emerging before winter and being killed by frost.)

Other species germinate better with a little bottom heat and the propagators described in Chapter Two will provide this. If you are in any doubt about seed and are not sure how to treat it for best results, try the combination of the following conditions that goes closest to what you know of the plant's natural habitat. Thus, if the seed is from an Asian paeony which grows wild in the Himalayas, the chances are it needs a vicious winter – hence, the primula treatment mentioned above would probably suit it. With the Mexican native *Salvia patens*, on the other hand, a warm bottom and protection from temperatures below 10°C – i.e. greenhouse plus heat – is the best bet:

Bottom Heat	No Heat
Spring	Autumn
Pans (trays)	Open ground
Greenhouse	Cold frame

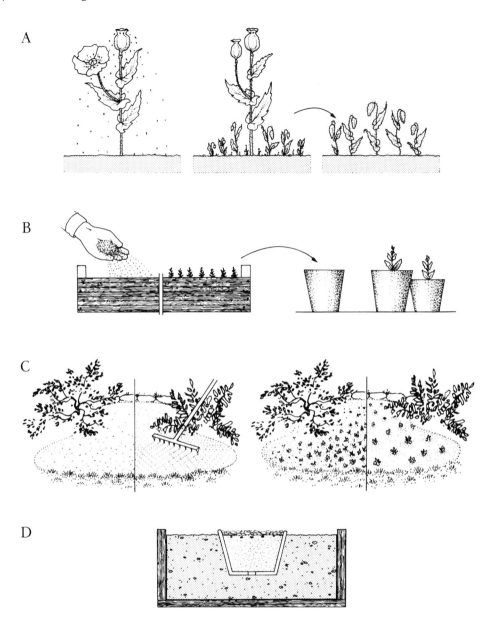

Fig. 18 Annuals – methods of propagation
A Self-growing: watch for seeds germinating; lift seedlings and transplant or thin out
B Trays: sowing into trays; pricking out into pots
C Ground: scatter onto clean ground; rake; thin if necessary
D Long-term germination—tree or paeony, 1–2 years – germination frame (section)

Dividing seed into four lots will enable you to sow some indoors and some outdoors in spring and autumn. That way, the bets are hedged and you are more likely to produce the plants you want.

Summary

1. Sow seed as fresh as possible

2. Primulas, meconopsis and other plants from temperate regions need vernalisation – sow and expose pans to frost

3. Use a simple propagator to provide bottom heat

4. Split sowing of unfamiliar species betwen heated and unheated conditions

CHAPTER SIX

Laissez-faire Rock Gardens

As any experienced gardener knows, rock gardens mean work. The great rockwork edifices in the early years of this century soon lost favour when gardeners' wages grew to more than a handful of loose change each week. As the numbers of gentlemen of leisure declined after the First World War, these fake alpine ranges dwindled in numbers until, today, the only gardens that have them are so flush with funds and labour that the enormous number of man hours, not to mention the cost of rebuilding every few decades, fits snugly into their budgets. The trouble is, once we have wandered over the realistic fake mountainside at Wisley or nearly broken our necks jumping off a limestone crag in the Cambridge Botanic Garden, we are so taken with the beauty and variety of the alpine plants growing among the rocks that we long to have some of them in our gardens. As it happens, though hardly *laissez-faire*, there are ways in which we can enjoy alpines without having to slave over a hard alp all day.

Somebody, very ill-informed and clearly not a real gardener, said recently that the trouble with English gardening was that the English had too much love for their plants. But he had missed the point by a good distance. Gardens need not be extensions of houses and the constraints on garden design and colour are not at all similar to constraints on interior decor. For a start, unless you decide to remodel the sky and exclude everything with green leaves, you have less control over colour than you think. Furthermore, when you wallpaper a room and hang a flight of pot ducks or a Rembrandt etching on your wall, they stay put unless you move them. Gardens are not like that! Not only do they change shape every day; they also change colour – all the time. The English gardening style, seen at its best in such places as Sissinghurst, depends every bit as much on plants as on structures. Indeed, the very strength of our better gardens lies in their planting within the context of carefully designed layout. If you don't believe me, imagine Sissinghurst without any plants – other than grass and a little carpet bedding along the walls and paths. Dullsville!

But, there are those rabid collectors among us gardeners who are obsessive about how many saxifrages or rose varieties they have in their possession but don't really care what their gardens actually look like. When you visit them, the chances are, you'll be treated to a two-hour lecture, with examples growing at your feet, on a narrow range of plants. The whole time might be spent looking at no more than a small area of the garden; or even the ground you are standing by and where some of the treasures are in yoghurt pots and others have inverted jam jars over them to keep the sparrows off.

What joy it is, then, to meet the able and knowledgeable plant lover who is also imbued with artistic talent and design flair. Such people, especially if they are catholic in their taste and know exactly how to grow the plants they like, are as precious to horticulture as Mozart is to music. If you are stirred by a deep affection for plants, the chances are, even though time never hangs heavy on your hands, you will want to grow some alpines somewhere in your garden.

Alpines

Alpines need not be confined to rock gardens and, though many of the most attractive are more suitable for growing under glass, the choice of excellent plants that thrive on neglect is still pretty wide. Rock gardens themselves can be designed for minimum maintenance, though part of the skill here lies in careful planting. The number of other garden sites suitable for alpines and small perennials is much larger than you might think. Where space is at a premium, every path can be used to house plants as well as to walk on. Steps, ledges, paved areas, walls, border fronts and even the bases of trees provide opportunities for small plants. In larger gardens, terraced beds or retaining walls can be built to hold alpines or limited rockwork can be incorporated into the gravel garden. Even a tiny yard can be furnished with one or more containers – stone troughs, fake tufa sinks or even concrete structures – all suitable for rock garden plants.

Fig. 19 Alpines
A Young healthy plant; old straggly plant; outer crown cut away, promotes new growth
B *Daphne cneorum*: young healthy plant; old straggly plant; soil covering heart of plant prompts new growth

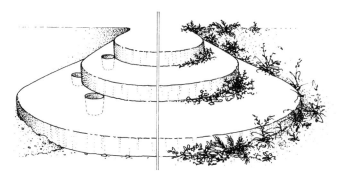

Fig. 20 Concrete steps: built-in pockets for planting; side-planting to soften hard edges

Easy propagation

Several alpines are easy to propagate, but be prepared to ring the changes with new plants.

Seed can be collected and sown. However, short cuts to propagation may well have more appeal unless you are a budding alpine gardener. Most plants that develop multiple rosettes will split with ease. The leathery leaved primulas – auriculas and smaller species – will grow quickly from side shoots, pulled off as soon after flowering as possible, and planted either in gritty compost or even straight into free-draining ground. If the side shoots have a root or two on them, so much the better. Spring flowering gentians will usually split easily in September and seem to flower more readily if they split frequently. Cyclamen on the other hand will not split easily. Their corms grow bigger by the year, some species growing 1 ft (0.3 m) across, but the only way they can be propagated safely is by seed – self-sown or collected and sown in gravelly compost in the cold frame.

The amount of time devoted to propagating alpines depends on your personal inclination – it can become an all-consuming hobby (especially if you get badly smitten and join the Alpine Garden Society). But, even if you limit yourself to plants which are mainly self-maintaining there is still a bewildering multitude of species and varieties from which to choose. New introductions are rolling in every month so there will never be an excuse for having a dull selection.

Some of the different ways in which alpines can be grown without trouble are described below, but the main point to remember is not to limit them to rock gardens. There are planting opportunities everywhere!

Traditional rockeries

Let us first give the rock garden a brief inspection. As far as appearance is concerned, the rule seems to be 'the bigger the stones, the better it looks'. Going into design in detail is beyond our brief but the 'plum pudding' style where a heap of soil has a few stones pushed into it to separate the aubrietas is not really a rock garden. Imitating the natural strata of the rocks, laying the stones to give the impression of the kind of natural rockscape you might find halfway up an alp is all very fine in theory but not always possible to execute. Using large slabs of block-shaped pieces, partially inserted into the side of a slope will go some way towards achieving a natural look. A bank or steep slope can have stone built into its side in a stepped arrangement, or soil can be held back at different levels by terracing. As with gravel (see Chapter Three) the use of local stone, where this is available, saves on haulage and is more likely than imported material to look as though it belongs in your landscape.

As with mixed borders and gravel gardens, perennial weeds are the biggest threat to rock gardens. A clean, healthy site is a must. Elimination of weeds is more difficult here than anywhere else, because once creeping rootstocks have penetrated the ground under the rocks they are almost impossible to get at. Applications of weedkiller may go some way towards killing them; however, the chances are a drop or two will fall on the wrong plant so that your favourite alpine turns yellow and keels over while the bindweed flourishes nearby. On rock gardens, because any form of mechanisation and even hand hoeing is impossible, annual weeds can also develop into serious trouble-makers. The smaller they are, the worse they are. Hairy bittercress, *Cardamine hirsuta*, is a scourge, seeding itself everywhere and, it seems, flowering within days of sowing. On rockwork, it can ruin everything if not weeded out before seeding. It can grow just big enough to seed in the harshest conditions so a tiny plant less than 1 in (2.5 cm) high can produce fifty or so babies within a month.

Planting for maximum effect with alpines is not difficult. The problem is never what to grow but what to leave out. With *laissez-faire* gardening in mind, certain varieties must be eliminated at once. Anything not suited to your soils or climate must go. Anything delicate enough to need protection from excessive damp in winter or cool shade in summer needs careful scrutiny. If you live in a damp area where winters are long but not deeply frosty, autumn gentians, petiolarid primulas and possibly even shortias are worth a try because they are so beautiful. Anywhere else, don't bother. They'll give you nothing but heartache but, even where Siberian winds cut through your February gardens for weeks on end, driving temperatures down to deep-freeze levels, you can still plant European rock primulas or spring gentians and will be staggered at how such apparently frail flowers manage, not only to survive but to flourish in the bracing environment. At the other extreme, anything too invasive should be kept out or reserved for areas where it can romp about without treading on any toes. New Zealand burrs (acaenas), for example, are not rock garden plants. Aubrieta, perhaps despised because it is so common, is rather invasive but easily controlled. I prefer the bad old purple-blue form to the fancy reds and dislike the variegated leaf form. There are double varieties but not so pretty as the double rock cress *Arabis caucasica* 'Flore-pleno'. Advantages of such commonplace plants are that they flower early in the year, establish quickly, and are loved by butterflies such as orange tips and over-wintered small tortoiseshells and peacocks. At the beginning of a rock garden's life, you can be heavy handed with these plants, putting them all over at first but cutting down their numbers when you have some choice specimens later on.

Spring is prime time for alpines. The number of good rock plants that flower later in summer is more limited but there are still plenty. Alpine pinks, certain campanulas, sisyrinchiums, a few of the sedums, rock roses, armeria, thymes, several geraniums, origanums and some polygonums are all examples of genera to take the seasons through to autumn. Bulbs play an important part and will be discussed later (see Chapter Nine). They provide some of the winter colour but you will also need evergreens and some plants that have interesting twigs or winter flowers. In acid areas, there are plenty of dwarf rhododendrons to consider. The native European alpenrose, *Rhododendron ferrugineum* is summer flowering and deep pink but most dwarf species flower in spring. *R. calostrotum* 'Gigha', for example, has wine-red flowers in April; some of the *R. yakushimanum* hybrids will delight rhodo fans by having large flowers on small shrubs but in more discriminating circles, the smaller violet-blue flowers of *R. scintillans* in mid-spring might have more appeal. Several daphnes make good evergreen shrublets, particularly *D. collina* which has purplish pink flowers in spring and the slightly larger *D. tangutica* with good green leaves and purple backed, white flowers followed by red berries. Dwarf willows have pleasant winter twiglets and some have lovely catkins. The choice of willows is vast but *Salix hylamatica* from Asia is covered with tiny pinkish red catkins in mid-spring, *S. grahami* develops a criss-crossed web of twiggy growth and has cool, dark-green leaves. Two silver-leaved willows need considering here too: *S. helvetica* has pale-green winter twigs and thin, silver leaves and *S. lanata* has rounded leaves covered with white wool. The foregoing gives a brief sketch of the sorts of alpine plants available but the best way to decide what to grow is to look at other people's rock gardens and to try some of the plants that appeal to you. Remember to steel yourself to dig them up and throw them away if, after all, you decide that they do not fit in with your planting scheme.

Summary

1. Rock gardens make work

2. Large rocks usually look better. Less soil equals less work

3. Alpines can be grown without rock gardens: in paths; on terraces; at the bases of trees; in dry or decaying stone walls; in border fronts; in alpine frames; in raised beds and in gravel

4. Before laying a new rock garden, make sure the site is clean and weed-free

5. Remember winter effects: twigs, evergreens, winter flowers

6. Limit your choice to plants that look after themselves

7. Start with rapid developers like aubrieta while the choice material develops. Don't be afraid to alter plantings as and when you consider necessary

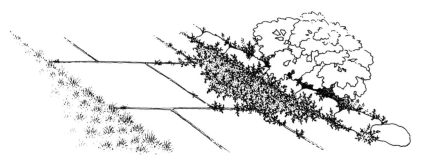

Fig. 21 Siting ground cover: invasive plants for paths

If, as is quite likely, the prospect of constructing a large rock garden fills you with dread, there is still no need to forgo collecting alpines or small plants. They have so many other places to grow that the choice is almost as varied without a rock garden as with one. Alpines can almost be considered as garnishes on the overall garden design.

Alternative rockeries

Pads, paths and paving

'Pad' is a Lincolnshire term for path. It's the bit that gets padded down along the side of the vegetable garden or leads from the road to the front door – often the same thing in Lincolnshire! Studied closely, it becomes apparent that the parts of the path that actually get trodden on are really quite limited. An 18 in (46 cm) catwalk does not leave much room for anything other than feet but if your paths are built with a generous width, a good many plants will grow happily in among the paving. Likewise, paved terraces will invariably have 'dead' areas where feet never go and where plant communities can be initiated. If new paths and paving are to be laid and plants are encouraged in them, certain considerations must be borne in mind. Nothing will grow in pure concrete and overall establishment is easier if the path overlies soil. However, soil in close contact with concrete and cement will amplify frost damage and could cause slabs or stones to work loose. A useful compromise can be worked out by having hardcore under the wearing part of the path but making sure that there are plenty of areas where planting will be possible.

Where paving slabs are to be laid, a level underlay of dry sand/cement (5:1) mix is advisable. The slabs can then be laid on blobs of cement. If gaps of up to 1 in (2.5 cm) are left between the slabs, sand/cement mix should be brushed into these to ensure a reasonably firm set. Plants or seeds can then be introduced and will usually grow satisfactorily in spite of the cement. If you plan to lay a solid sheet of concrete, rather than slabs, insert stakes or logs at intervals – not regular – so that, when these are removed, cavities are there ready to receive the plants. With crazy paving, be sure to leave a good number of crevices and chinks to be used later as plant receptacles.

When money is tight, there is a crafty way of imitating paving slabs. The technique is to lay concrete, level it and then to insert thin laths of wood at right-angles before it

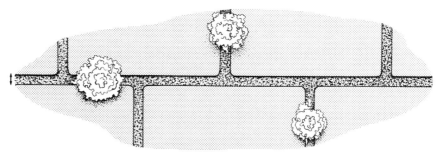

Fig. 22 Paving: slab laying, leaving space for planting

sets. They will form rectangles and squares – you can decide whether to make them regular sizes or to vary them. (They tend to look less fake if they are all different sizes.) As soon as the concrete has gone off, remove the laths carefully, without chipping the edges and then, brush the surfaces vigorously with a stiff bristle or wire brush, concentrating on all the rough edges. Within a year, the resulting path will mellow, grow lichen and look almost like stone paving. Planting into this will not be possible unless specific holes have been left through to the bottom but if the 'cracks' left behind after removing the laths are deep enough, plants like houseleeks and stonecrop may well take hold. Many sedums, including Britain's native biting stone crop, *Sedum acre* are charming plants which delight in furnishing otherwise barren wastes.

Paving slabs or flagstones make good stepping stones set into gravel. (See Chapter Three.)

Steps

One of the joys of Beth Chatto's garden in Essex is the way in which she has furnished her steps. Any garden that has different levels is likely to be more interesting than having everything on one plane so, wherever it is practicable to create terracing or to accentuate the difference between one level and another, even if a bout of heavy engineering is involved, the matter is worth consideration. To connect different levels, you'll need steps or a slope. The cheapest steps are made from concrete moulded with

Fig. 23 Rock steps (section): stepped embankment; faked dry-stone wall

shuttering. However, stone flags or blocks can be used in formal settings or, in more rustic situations, logs can be set into the ground horizontally to retain the soil. The resulting terracing makes a passable staircase.

The starkness of newly set cement can soon be offset by planting the edges of steps and corners with spreading plants – preferably evergreens. Several varieties of thyme will intermingle to form a fragrant staircarpet – what does it matter if part of it gets walked on? The aroma of crushed thyme leaves will add to the pleasure of strolling through the garden. If the concrete ends, on either side, with a slope down into soil, planting is facilitated. Besides thyme, for full sun, trailing cotoneasters such as *C. dammeri* 'Radicans' or *C. microphyllus* will cover the ground rapidly, hugging the contours as it goes. Low conifers such as *Juniperus conferta* are equally speedy and in shade, periwinkles provide rapid cover. Slightly taller edging shrubs will allow climbers to be planted amongst them. All the *Clematis viticella* hybrids are suitable for this because they can be cut to ground level every February and are therefore unlikely to get big enough to become untidy. The inevitable spaces and bare patches make perfect spots for a variety of little alpines which will produce splashes of colour or points of interest. People are fond of pausing on stairs, indeed, those who are a little unsteady on their pins might want to take a while to negotiate as few as three of four steps. The chance of stopping to admire something special will make the garden more memorable. In dappled shade, for instance, the little arum *Arisarum proboscideum* appeals to children, and to the child in all of us, because the flowers look like hordes of naughty, long-tailed mice scampering about among the bottle-green foliage. For the more aesthetically minded, something striking like a brilliant magenta erodium or a mysteriously marked fritillary might make a greater impression. The choice is nearly infinite and for variety, you can ring the changes with speedy results whenever you fancy.

Sinks and troughs

In the *laissez-faire* garden, containers need to be virtually self-maintaining, needing no more than an occasional weed out or clear out. In high summer, they will dry right through unless they are watered and so, either a regular soak is required or they must be planted with subjects that do not object to hot dry conditions. The Mediterranean coast is full of such plants but in August, botanically speaking, it is dull as ditchwater. Most small bulbs disappear in early summer and the little maquis orchids, cyclamen, anemones and irises go with them. Rock roses and lavenders are usually too big and untidy so, inevitably, the sink gardens will look their best in spring but lose some of their appeal in late summer.

When selecting containers, the ideal is to go for the biggest you can accommodate. The larger the volume of soil, the longer moisture is retained and therefore the wider the range of plants you can use. Although you are likely to compose a picture with mixed planting, it is worth remembering that with some species, a single plant may be very effective. A small limestone sink containing nothing but *Salix reticulata* or perhaps nothing more than an encrustation of houseleeks can be very effective. Single dwarf shrubs look delightful when strategically placed. There's a tiny holly – *Ilex aquifolium* 'Hascombensis' – which has small, shiny green leaves and grows into a pleasing little mound. Willows, the short, stubby kinds, have the added advantage of looking different in different seasons. *Salix boydii* is the stubbiest, looking old and gnarled before it has reached a height of 6 in (15.2 cm).

Such plants are also valuable anchor points for mixed plantings in troughs and sinks. One's natural instinct is to try to create a garden in miniature. Tiny trees – almost bonsai – go in amid strategically placed rocks. Then we plant bulbs and even the scillas tower over the tree-tops making the whole affair look out of proportion. The other mistake is to plant 'dwarf conifers' which soon spoil the whole thing by reaching 5 ft (1.5 m) and starving everything else out. An annual review is necessary. The fun of sink gardening is that most of the occupants will take quite happily to transplanting. The confines of the container mean that you are unlikely to slice through an important tap root. Even the anchor plants, if they seem to be growing too slowly or too big, can be moved and replaced with something else.

Some evergreen material is essential, particularly if the container is near the house or likely to be seen frequently. Besides *I. aquifolium* 'Hascombensis' some other small species of holly make worthwhile container plants. *Ilex crenata* has tiny, waxy leaves and can either be clipped like a diminutive hedge or left to grow into a stubby shrublet. There are several cultivars with differing characteristics, all of which make good companions for plants with good winter twigs or catkins. Dwarf azaleas on acid soils, provided they don't dry too much in summer, produce colour at the right time and the smaller daphnes, particularly *D. cneorum* make trusty subjects for limy gardens. Many daphnes reputed to dislike alkaline soil grow well on my limestone but *D. odora* hates it.

Having placed the anchors, filling up the rest is easy. Most bulbs will appreciate conditions in sinks and are described later. (See Chapter Nine) Since the majority flower in spring, it is no bad plan to leave that season to them and concentrate on herbaceous plants for later. Anything that fails to stay small and tidy is likely to spoil the whole sink. Plants with a lot of flower to little leaf are usually more welcome – small pinks such as 'Waithmans Beauty' or 'Pikes Pink', parahebes, the exquisite *Geranium farreri* which has sugar-pink petals and chocolate stamens – anything that will elicit an Ooh! or an Ah! from the visitor. On the subject of chocolate, there is a small columbine, *Aquilegia viridiflora* which will grow happily in a sink and is certain

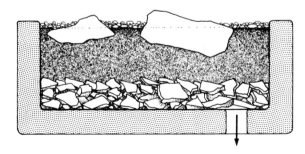

Fig. 24 Sink garden (section)

to be a conversation piece. The petals are dark-brown and green – just like a chocolate mint!

Strategic stones or lumps of tufa can give a sink more contour and, if there is room, some kind of dip or valley down the middle may look fine but one must avoid straying towards prissiness. Limiting the number of species to no more than half-a-dozen, but having good, established clumps of each can make a better show than a miscellany of immature plants. There will be mistakes in planting – there always are – but these can be put right once they have become apparent. We tend to regard planting with any form of perennial or shrub to be irrevocable simply because such plants last for more than a season. This is far too style-cramping an attitude and it does not take long to discover just how easily things move, even when they are quite mature. With shrubs, unless they are excessively slow growing, the safest bet is to prune as much off the top as you think you've damaged at the root.

Summary

1. Lay new paving with plants in mind. Introduce them by forcing young plants between the cracks or by spreading seed over the paving and brushing it into them

2. Furnish the edges of garden steps with ground huggers

3. Plant sinks with 'anchor' plants but ring the changes if anything gets out of hand or boring

CHAPTER SEVEN

Laissez-faire Roses

An English garden without roses is hard to imagine. Indeed, wherever there are gardens in the world, the chances are, roses will be planted. Delicate hybrid teas roast away in the white-hot summers of Wagga Wagga or shiver in Reykjavik. Often, they are overused – few public parks are without their beds of floribundas and, in Aberdeen, there is a small hillock planted with 96,000 of them. Old roses have enjoyed an international revival which began some 40 years ago and has gathered momentum ever since. Thanks to enthusiasts like Vita Sackville-West, Hilda Murrell and Graham Stuart Thomas, many varieties threatened with extinction before the Second World War are now cultivated in healthy numbers all over the temperate world.

Name a spot and there is a rose variety suited for it. One kind or another will flourish practically anywhere. Most are hardy enough to take months of frost, some will climb to the top of a 30 ft (9.1 m) tree, others will sit in a container flowering all summer but never reaching more than 18 in (45.7 cm). There are varieties in flower from May to Christmas; others last a fortnight. Some have magnificent fruits, making a valuable contribution to autumn colour; some even have aromatic foliage.

The kind of rose not to grow in the *laissez-faire* garden is the kind that needs pruning in March, deadheading, spraying every fortnight and feeding with a manure mulch in spring followed by at least one extra boost of fertiliser in summer. Meaning that, unless you like the colours of such varieties as 'Superstar', 'Whisky Mac', 'Dearest' or 'Evelyn Fison' so much that you are prepared to work extra hard, they are not for you. But these varieties flower for so long! Can you hope to have such an extended flowering season but use easier roses? The answer is 'yes and no'! Yes, there are plenty of roses that look after themselves, repeat flower and need minimal pruning but, no, there is nothing like the range of colours and nothing flowers quite so copiously as a modern hybrid when it is healthy. Thus, for certain colours you may be obliged to rely on modern hybrids.

Colour

The colour range with roses is broad. Few of the older varieties have hard reds or yellows in their make up; few moderns have that soft, watery quality and texture of petal that lends so much to the appeal of old roses. There are species with startling displays for a fortnight that would be uncomfortable for longer. 'Canary Bird', for instance, is the kind of obtrusive yellow that is welcome in late spring but when the summer flowers are coming out one is usually glad to see the back of it. Because they are almost always planted with other things, perpetual roses must be of a colour to suit their companions from June to October. The harsher colours are not necessarily wrong in this context but may not be so easy to blend with the supplementary planting. With shorter-lived varieties, harmony is as important but mistakes are apparent for a much shorter time and colour matching is easier. Some plants have a 'safe' colour which seems reasonably restful with virtually all roses. Lavenders belong with them, not only when their flowers contrast but also when their young growth looks such a soft green against the liverish red of the emerging rose foliage and later, when they turn silver grey, toning down some of the brighter rose flower colours. Geraniums (cranesbills – not pelargoniums) often associate well because of their blue flowers and the lime green ladies' mantle *Alchemilla mollis*, itself a rose relative, is a fitting plant with which to furnish the feet of shrub roses. In mixed borders and other parts of the garden where, though not playing a lead role, roses are nevertheless present, close attention must be paid to colour because with such showy flowers, a clash would be amplified.

General care

Before describing the delights of individual roses, we should look first at the work involved. With *laissez-faire* roses, this is kept to a minimum but certain routine tasks are unavoidable if we want good results. Listed here, these may appear burdensome, but, in practice, through the gardening year, the time spent working on your roses will be considerably less than the time you will be able to spend enjoying them.

Buying stock

The most meticulous aftercare will be fruitless unless you start with well-grown, correctly named stock. Since roses are on sale more or less everywhere, the chances of

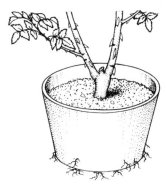

Fig. 25 Points to look out for when buying roses: healthy top growth; roots filling pot but not pot-bound

buying dud plants are fairly high. As a great believer in specialist nurseries, I prefer to deal direct with the growers. There are several, nowadays, which specialise in old and new shrub roses and which supply by mail order. Getting out and about in summer, notebook and pen at the ready, enables you to decide which roses to have in your garden by looking at them in the flesh.

If garden centres appeal to you, some of the better ones have good stocks of roses in containers. Look for signs of healthy growth and, if recently potted up, beware of over-pruned roots which might slow down the rate at which the plants will take off. Potted shrubs, especially pot-bound specimens need watering frequently – sometimes twice a day – while they await planting and, in every case, should be planted as soon as possible after purchase. Buying roses at a supermarket or garage makes about as much sense as bringing ham sandwiches to a barmitzvah. Such wares are set out to be bought on impulse. Not part of the well-planned garden!

Planting and feeding

The best time to plant is winter. There is no special mystery to rose planting – just dig a hole and shove the roots into it, heeling the soil down firmly. A scattering of slow release fertiliser – sterilised bone meal, for example – will benefit the plant and, in excessively limy areas, a tonic of chelated iron might improve the growth rate. It is important to make sure that all the roots are buried and that the base of the plant sits at ground level. Planting too deeply can cause a briar problem but having the crown proud of the ground results in wind-rock and collapsible plants. Once the rose is in, go over it with secateurs, removing any broken or misshapen branches. Even if the plant is perfect, pruning about a third of the top growth away is good policy because it eases the strain on the damaged root system in the first few months. Subsequent feeding is important but very easy. In my own garden I merely hurl a general fertiliser – containing 15 per cent each of nitrogen, phosphorus and potassium – about randomly until my arm aches too much to throw any more. (The target rate is a spread of about 2 oz per sq yd (58 g per sq m). The roses get an extra handful round their bases and also a two-yearly mulch of compost, laid on in late winter. (See Chapter Two.) The whole business takes no more than an hour or two each year, though a heavy mulch can be more laborious. In summer, if the roses are flagging a little, I mix a foliar feed in with the fungicide spray. The resulting greenness of the leaves may be in my mind's eye rather than in fact, though!

A couple of years ago, Britain suffered from an unusually vicious and prolonged winter. By North American standards it would have been considered mild but for us it spelt disaster, killing off so many plants previously considered hardy. Unlike those of the northern United States and Canada, British winters are followed by cool summers. The year in question had no summer at all really, it just edged its way from bitter cold to wet and chilly, had a five-day heat wave when temperatures rocketed to nearly 70°F (21°C) and then went to dreary autumn again. The result was that all the winter-damaged material sulked during summer because growing conditions were so poor. Foliar feed seemed to help the roses a great deal that year when some – the hybrid musks, for

15. Stepping stones make walking on grit more pleasant.

16. *Laissez-faire* planting but a strict colour
     scheme—blue and yellow.

17. Tree paeonies and columbines—a
happy association.

18. Snowdrops and *Cyclamen coum* begin
   the year's display.

example – had been killed to ground level. The message behind this rambling story is that in times of stress, extra feed can help.

Pruning

The modern hybrids need pruning every year – preferably once in autumn and again, properly, in March. With most shrub roses, the approach is different. Some, especially where they are to be allowed complete freedom of growth, may not need touching at all. Others need checking over every couple of years just to prune out any old, dying or dead wood. Repeat flowerers need more diligent pruning and, by cutting hard after the first flowers, many can be induced to climax in autumn. Alternatively, light deadheading will result in sporadic blooming right through the season.

Certain shrub roses that flower once only can be treated exactly as raspberry canes. The year's flower stems are all removed in November, leaving the vegetative stems for the next year. These will break into blooming sprays more readily if they are bent or tied-in in some way. At Sissinghurst, the wands are tied down at the ends, resulting in bowed stalks which break into flower along their whole length. Taller growing plants such as 'Ispahan' can be tied in a spiral arrangement round three or four posts. Time consuming work, this, but worthwhile if you have a single plant in a key position.

By far the most laborious annual pruning task is with the climbers. These are the ones that double your chance of injury; not only from the thorns but also by your falling off the ladder when you attempt to train them! The perfect rosarian will have all his climbing roses trained into fan configurations by Christmas, every lead neatly tied-in so that no stems cross over. I always do an immaculate job with 'Zéphirine Drouhin' and 'Kathleen Harrop' because they are thornless. But try the same degree of perfectionism with 'Mermaid' which bristles with hooked stilettos and you end up feeling like the victim of a chainsaw massacre. *Laissez-faire* gardeners can allow many of the ramblers to swarm up trees unaided or to slump informally over low walls. All you need, in these cases, is to remove any dead wood within your reach and occasionally, stretch a wire over the top just to keep it down – strong wind can sometimes lift the whole plant off a wall. On a high wall or the side of a house, more

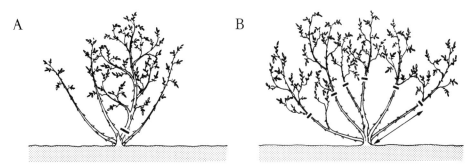

Fig. 26 Pruning shrub roses
A Pruning old flowering stems
B Pruning long growth back to 3 ft (1 m) every third year

careful training is desirable. With ramblers, the best policy is to cut anything more than a year old to the ground as described for some of the shrub roses. Every year, provided the plant is healthy, a good half-a-dozen strong leads will have developed and these are so much easier to tie-in than last year's growth. Flowering will be more profuse but in poor years, if there are too few new leads, the best of the old ones must be pruned to the main stem and tied-in alongside.

There are several nearly thornless ramblers including 'Goldfinch' and 'Veil-chenblau' which look interesting grown together. The former is apricot in the bud, fading to cream and the latter a rather disturbing purple – the colour of raw muscle – with a white and yellow centre.

Pests and diseases

Roses are disease prone. Some are hardy enough to be able to live with infections and flower well enough even though they may become progressively disfigured as the season advances. For others, something as commonplace as blackspot can prove fatal. Organic gardeners who do not allow themselves any form of chemical control will be handicapped in their rose growing but will still be able to enjoy an interesting number of resistant and vigorous varieties.

If, like me, you dislike using chemicals but resort to it in extreme situations, rose growing is made much easier. Preventive spraying is more effective than shotgun treatments but need not mean heavy chemical consumption. Ideally, say the fungicide manufacturers, spraying should be repeated every ten to fourteen days. In practice, I have found it possible to achieve reasonable control of both mildew and black spot without spraying more often than about once in three or four weeks. Susceptible varieties will show symptoms before that but these could be given an interim treatment. I use a variety of systemic products, with heavy dependence on benomyl.

Insecticides are harder to justify and are, potentially, more threatening to the wildlife population. From time to time, a disastrous plague of greenfly descends and multiplies among the roses and, at that time, some form of control becomes essential. I would like to profess innocence and suggest that I only employ soap suspensions or organic concoctions but have to admit to using the systemic insecticide dimethoate. The idea is that the chemical is absorbed into the plant so that the piercing, sucking insects drink affected juice and die. It works. But is it also transferred to nectar and pollen so that bees and butterflies can ingest it? I have never observed dead bees or butterflies after spraying, and I try not to spray when they are on the wing so perhaps it isn't, but I have to admit to a mildly troubled conscience.

The level of prophylaxis you adopt will depend on your pesticide philosophy. Keeping sprays to the minimum makes some ecological sense: growing only resistant varieties and species makes even more.

Propagating

Far and away the best method of increasing your rose stocks is to buy more from the grower. Professionally-grown plants get off to a good start and are a lot less trouble

Fig. 27 Rose propagation – propagation of suckers (for roses on their own roots only)

than trying to raise your own unless you develop an interest in budding. If you do, this book, burgeoning with valuable information though it undoubtedly is, will not be able to help you! The author has never budded a rose – or anything else – in his life and refuses to write about anything he has not personally experienced.

One infuriating aspect of commercially-grown roses is that they are nearly all grafted onto a different stock. Understandable though this is for hybrids that might not grow very well on their own roots, for most of the rampant shrub roses it is quite unnecessary. Grown from your own cuttings, vigorous roses will never produce briars and will grow just as lustily as their grafted parents. The easiest way to root cuttings is to push prunings of young growths into the ground in a sheltered corner and then to forget about them until the following season. In good conditions, a 70 per cent take is the norm, so from a few cuttings you will be able to produce more roses than you need. Any variety of known vigour will strike this way and even the more effete hybrids will often take root, though the resulting plants will be different in character from their grafted parents – usually smaller and more straggly.

Species can be raised from seed and, wherever a self-sown seedling turns up – a frequent occurrence in the *laissez-faire* garden – be sure to let it flower before you expel it. The rose 'Arthur Hillier' turned up this way in its namesake's arboretum and I have a pleasing selection of *Rosa moyesii* seedlings growing along the side of a hideous old shed. They are not really marketable shrubs but make a delightful show twice a year. (Flowers and hips.) Waiting for seed to germinate can be time consuming and the safest method of sowing seems to be to wash off the pulp and place the seeds in drills in the garden. They may take a long time to come but, when they do, it will be another two years, at least, before they flower.

Old roses often sucker. The old gallicas are good at this and the burnet roses too prolific, turning a bare patch into a bristling, impenetrable thicket in a couple of seasons. I've even seen them forcing their way up through an asphalt pavement. Suckers pulled out in midwinter and transplanted will grow away rapidly. They should be cut hard back after planting to promote branching and care is needed to avoid making the mistake of transplanting samples of the grafting stock rather than the variety. The difference is usually easy to see but less so in winter and in any case, some of the old roses look a bit like briars.

Summary

1. Buy roses from specialist growers. Make your selection by looking at, and smelling, the flowering plants the season before

2. Feed with general fertiliser or bone meal on planting and thereafter once a year, in spring, with compound fertiliser or a natural melange such as blood, fish and bonemeal (pay attention to hygiene)

3. Rotted manure or other mulching material helps, especially on thin soils. Roses love heavy soil that stays moist

4. No need to over-prune *laissez-faire* roses but cut out dead or old wood

5. Adopt minimal disease control methods, or grow only resistant varieties

6. The best way to multiply roses is to buy more from the grower

Purpose planting

Having heard the worst about the work involved with them, we can turn next to look at the multitude of garden uses roses can be put to. More often than not, they are grown in mixed company rather than on their own. Even traditional rose gardens usually have companion plants – they'd be so dull out of season if they didn't!

Giant shrub roses can be splendid in isolation. A friend planted two or three on the far side of a field which was adjacent to her garden boundary. 'We're extending into that field,' she told me, 'and I wanted something to entice visitors over there.' It was a clever move. Left unpruned but growing in good soil, certain shrub roses reach heights of 10 ft (3.0 m) or more and may spread a similar distance across. Species like *R. moyesii* will do this and so will some of the hybrid musks – especially 'Buff Beauty', 'Cornelia' (dark pink buds opening to apricot pink flowers) and 'Felicia' (salmon pink). *Rosa sericea* 'Pteracantha' has unexciting white flowers but great wands armed with the most fierce-looking thorns imaginable. These are transluscent and russet-red in early summer, drying to beige in winter. A lovely plant but fains I prune it! The irony is that, to ensure really good new growths, the old wood needs cutting back every year.

Old repeaters

There are three popular myths about old roses. They run something like this:

1. They never need pruning
2. They get no disease
3. They only flower for a short time

Disease and pruning we have already discussed and applies as much to the old shrub roses as to their modern counterparts. Many are disease resistant but others need protection from fungal problems. As for flowering, the gallicas, the albas, the centifolias and damasks only flower once but china roses, hybrid musks, several bourbons, hybrid perpetuals and one or two other old-fashioned plants repeat with varying degrees of prolificacy. The colour range among the nineteenth-century varieties is more subtly graded than with modern roses – a lot of pinks in different intensities, plummy reds, soft whites with pink shading and the yellows limited to peach or apricot undertones. Besides colour, the petal texture and flower shapes vary far more than with modern roses. There are rounded blooms, hemispherical shapes, flowers with green buttons in their centres, semi-doubles, pointed 'hybrid tea' shaped buds and so on. But above all else, there is the heady, lazy scent. Walk into a garden of old roses on a still June evening and the atmosphere is almost intoxicating. Each variety has its own pattern of scents – some almost fruity, others with a spicy background, some faint but smelling clean and fresh and others so rich they overpower your olfactory equipment. Without doubt, scent is one of the most important dimensions of the rose and why modern breeders have paid that aspect so little attention remains a mystery. Could it be that they breed what we, the consumers, want and that the mass market demands screaming colours regardless of smell? Was 'Masquerade' with its clashing colours of near-red and near yellow, on one stem the apotheosis, or will there be something worse?

A garden of old roses, thoughtfully planted, will be nearly as colourful as a modern collection in September but the June climax will be more intense. Certain 'one-timers' are such good and useful plants that they must be included. After all, nobody complains about lilac or camellias and they only flower once. For *laissez-faire* treatment we are only interested in varieties that behave well, but if you become obsessed with the idea of collecting old roses you could begin to widen your scope. The roses listed below show a few examples of the many trouble-free varieties in cultivation today. They are divided into groups as follows:

Non-recurrents

Alba

All have fresh greenish-blue foliage, good vigour and seem not to be fussy about where they grow.

'**Alba Maxima**' The Jacobite rose. Vigorous shrub, excellent for hedging. Soft white, the petals approaching pink at their centres. Reasonable hips.

'**Maiden's Blush**' Similar in shape to 'Alba Maxima' but growing larger. The most exquisite blush pink flowers are semi-double and produced in great numbers. Heavily scented.

'**Félicité Parmentier**' Smaller than the other albas with greener leaves. The flowers are rounded in the bud opening flat but very double. The scent is strong and colour pale creamy pink.

Centifolia

'Fantin Latour' If I were only allowed one old rose, choosing between this and 'Rosa Mundi' would be difficult. The bush grows quite large – 5 ft (1.5 m) or more – and the stems arch gracefully. Glossy, darkish foliage makes a perfect foil for the pale blush-pink flowers which fade gracefully toward their edges as they age. They come in large clusters and are fun to pick because the stems are almost thornless. Graham Stuart Thomas states that 'Fantin Latour' is not the true name for this rose but that is what all the growers and gardeners call it. A rose by any other name . . .

Moss

Several old roses have mossed buds. As if that were not charm enough, they all smell exquisitely sweet and often grow from suckers.

'Old Pink Moss' There seems not to be a proper name for this small – it grows to about 4 ft (1.2 m) – shrub with heavily mossed buds through which the deep pink petals show. The scent is sweet and strong.

'William Lobb' Tall and untidy – almost growable as a climber but equally good falling about drunkenly at the back of the border. Named after the great Cornish plant collector but bred in France where it is called 'Duchesse d'Istrie'. The blooms, strongly scented, open the colour of vintage port and fade to rich plummy purple-mauve. The wonderfully velvet texture of the petals makes picking this rose worthwhile, even though the stems are massed with thorns and bristles.

Damask

'Ispahan' Far and away the best damask because it grows so vigorously and, though only once flowering, begins early and finishes late. Ideal candidate for the 'raspberry cane' treatment, flexing the new leads to make them flower along their length. Perfect for furnishing an arch because the wands grow to the right lengths for bending over the top without having to trim too much off. Strong, spicy fragrance, blush pink, middle-sized flowers on good clusters.

Gallica

Most people, when they imagine old roses, think of the gallicas. There are many still in cultivation of which all three below are excellent for the *laissez-faire* rosarian. Some of them sucker if grown on their own roots.

'Charles de Mills' Two strong points: flower shape and colour. Glowing crimson petals are tightly packed in a quartered design, making up a bud that opens to form an hemisphere and finally flattens to create a symmetrical rosette. Good scent, tidy habit.

'Rosa Mundi' A striped rose of great antiquity, streaks of light and dark pink on the flowers which are semi double and scented. At Kiftsgate it makes a splendid, low hedge. (A striped version of the Apothecary's Rose – *R. gallica.*)

'Tuscany Superb' Not dissimilar in shape and habit to 'Rosa Mundi' but rich claret red with golden central stamens.

Recurrents

As is so often repeated, the great disadvantage with the few roses just mentioned is that, like almost every other shrub known to man, they only flower once a year. Since roses are so heavily relied upon to hold planting schemes together and to contribute plenty of colour, the list continues with a few old roses that are reasonably easy to manage and are recurrent.

China roses

Also called 'monthly roses' because they flower every month. Several of these are in the breeding of our modern perpetual varieties.

'Hermosa' A small bush with successions of pink, rounded flowers. Not very vigorous but a faithful supplier of bloom. Grows to 3 ft (1 m). 'Old Blush' is similar.

'Cecile Brunner' Small, clean pink buds produced endlessly. A tidy grower but needing repeated deadheading to encourage new blooms. There is a climbing sort.

'Perle d'Or' Not vigorous, tiny flower buds, perfectly formed salmon pink and good for small indoor arrangements. The opened blooms are a little disappointing after such neat buds but it does flower until Christmas if the weather is reasonable.

Hybrid musks

Have you ever thought how much we gardeners owe to the clergy? In the days when vicars and rectors had energetic curates to do all the parish work, they were able to indulge in their hobbies without too many rude interruptions from their flocks. One such was the Reverend J.H. Pemberton who, in his Romford garden, bred some of our loveliest hybrid musk roses in the first quarter of this century. 'Cornelia' and 'Felicia' have already been mentioned but he gave us several others:

'Buff Beauty' Apricot fading to buffish cream. Large and fragrant.

'**Pax**' Cream white, also big and very recurrent. Its susceptibility to black spot tempts me to re-name it 'Pox'!

'**Penelope**' Still very popular because of its soft, peachy pink sprays and its reliability.

'**Prosperity**' Cream, fading white. The flowers are well formed and the colour deepens to lemon at their centres. The best scent of all the hybrid musks and a lovely colour to harmonise with dark blues.

Other recurrents

Though pitifully short, the list below provides suggestions for a score of old roses that could get you started on a new (old) rose garden.

Some old repeaters

'**Adam Messerich**' A Bourbon with strong pink flowers on quite a large shrub. The scent is supposed to be like raspberries.

'**Stanwell Perpetual**' Ferny foliage, inherited from the burnet roses in its ancestry, makes this a pleasing shrub. The flowers are white, colouring with a hint of pink as they age. It gets quite large – up to 6 ft (1.8 m) and flowers all the time.

'**Vick's Caprice**' An American plant bred in 1891. Boldly striped pink and lilac – more contrasted than 'Rosa Mundi' and, unlike her, repeats reasonably well but has a main flowering period in June.

Siting for colour

With careful siting, most of these grow in harmony together. There are no acid yellows or hard reds, since varieties with those colours came into cultivation more recently. Such shades are unlikely to belong among old varieties but, as long as you keep a careful watch on colour, there is no reason at all why you should not take full advantage of the many excellent modern roses available and interplant them with old ones. The difference in flower types is fascinating and certain moderns go particularly well with old roses. The German-bred white floribunda 'Iceberg' has a classic quality, as do big shrub roses like 'Nevada'. We owe the firm of W. Kordes a debt of gratitude for such varieties as 'Fritz Nobis', 'Scarlet Fire' and the 'Frühlings-' series, especially 'Frühlingsgold' because, unlike 'Iceberg' which is also from their stable, they are the perfect *laissez-faire* shrubs, thriving on neglect.

In recent years, in response to the revival of interest in old roses, the English breeder David Austin has come up with some original modern hybrids which have taken on all the good attributes of the old breeds but flower recurrently. There seem to be more each year and, though most of them have yet to stand the test of time, there is no mistaking their appeal. The colour range is broad and includes modern yellow in an old rose shape – 'Graham Thomas', mid pink – 'Warwick Castle', sombre red – 'Othello' and pale pinkish-white – 'Claire Rose'. The naming has been imaginative and leans heavily on Britain's half-timbered heritage with names like 'Mary Rose' (pale pink) named after Henry VIII's ship which was exhumed from the mud of the Solent in 1982, 'The Squire' (crimson) and 'Lordly Oberon' (pink) – though why 'lordly' and not 'jealous' for such a petulant fairy, heaven knows!

Most of these roses are likely to suffer from disease, some severely. The spraying regime has been described but a selection for organic gardeners now follows. Even these roses are, to a greater or lesser extent, susceptible to some form of disease but it is unlikely to damage them seriously.

Rugosas

By far the biggest group of roses that will cope without spraying are the rugosas. They are nearly all strongly scented, all flower recurrently and many have magnificent autumn fruits – great clusters of fleshy hips which sometimes appear together with the flowers. They are easy to grow from seed and an interesting colour range can be obtained that way. Most rugosa hybrids make good hedges which can be kept to a convenient size by trimming once a year. They sucker vigorously and are not difficult to root from cuttings. Though the pure species, *Rosa rugosa*, resists virtually all diseases, its hybrids may not be quite so tough because of the other roses in their breeding.

'Agnes' A Canadian introduction (1922) with soft amber-yellow, fragrant blooms. Vigorous to 8 ft (2.4 m) but inclined to be straggly.

'Blanc Double de Coubert' White, very double, very fragrant. Grows to 5 ft (1.5 m).

'Conrad F. Meyer' A great, rampaging shrub up to 8 ft (2.4 m) with masses of pale pink, fragrant blooms and healthy foliage.

'Frau Dagmar Hastrup' Single, clear pink flowers on a medium height bush. Good fruits.

'Mrs Anthony Waterer' Unique purple-red flowers produced all summer. Tall but graceful in its habit.

'Roseraie de l'Haÿ' Large and vigorous. Purple crimson flowers with superb scent. One of the most outstanding rugosas.

'Sarah van Fleet' One of the most prolific flowerers – clear pink and delightfully scented. Grows to 8 ft (2.4 m).

Other species and varieties for organic gardeners

Most of the true species will grow happily without any form of disease control. All the *Rosa moyesii* hybrids, sweetbriars, relatives of our native dog roses, burnet roses and *Rosa rubrifolia* are resistant. Here are some useful examples from these groups:

Burnet Rose *Rosa spinosissima*, the garden forms are double white, pink or yellow. All scented but not recurrent.

'Dunwich' A single cream form of the wild burnet rose.

'Nevada' Described earlier. There's a pink form, 'Marguerite Hilling' which is just as easy.

R. californica **'Plena'** Pink but not recurrent. Grows to 8 ft (2.4 m).

Sweetbriars *R. eglanteria* varieties. All have apple scented foliage. Examples are: 'Amy Robsart' – almost single, mid pink, large; 'Julia Mannering' – pale pink vigorous; 'Meg Merrilees' – rather a flat red but a good doer; 'Lord Penzance' – deliciously aromatic foliage, buff flowers.

R. × highdownensis Magnificent shrub with wine pink flowers and superb hips. Large and rapid.

R. roxburghii Odd, rather than beautiful, prickly with un-roselike foliage and extraordinary spiky hips.

'William III' A gorgeous deep pink burnet rose with paler petal backs, not very tall and with all the burnet attributes – ferny foliage, vigour and scent.

Hips

I have already mentioned *R. moyesii* and its hybrids which are especially lovely because of their elongated, fiery orange-red, flask shaped hips. Other good hip species are the sweetbriars listed above and some of the rampant ramblers, like *R. filipes* and *R. helenae* which produce clusters of tiny hips hanging almost like hawthorn fruits. *R. holodonta* has hips which are even longer and thinner than those of *R. moyesii* and the fruits of *R. andersonii* grow in upright clusters reminiscent of our own wild roses. (Do not despise native wild roses whose hips are both beautiful and popular with the resident wildlife.) The rugosas have been discussed along with the luscious fruiting *R. villosa* and the burnets which have intriguing little black fruits.

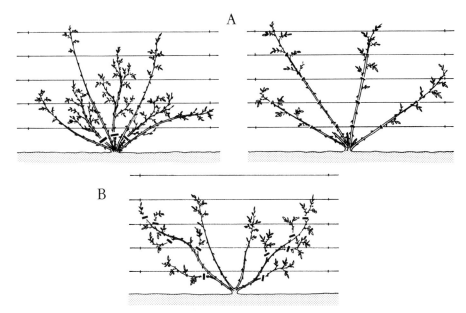

Fig. 28 Wall-trained roses – ramblers and climbers
A Rambler: prune out old wood; tie new growth
B Climber cut back to stimulate growth

Summary

Hopefully, the foregoing will have provided you with a smattering of ideas. There are plenty of other disease resistant roses and seeing as many as possible growing in other gardens will help you to discover what will suit your own.

Whatever your level of keenness as a gardener – whether you loathe gardening or love it – the chances are you will have a rose or two somewhere on your patch. Assuming you do grow roses, why not grow the best?

You may have noticed a glaring absence in this chapter. Apart from the rampant ramblers, we have barely mentioned climbers. These will be covered as part of the next chapter which is devoted to wall plants.

CHAPTER EIGHT

Wall Plants and Climbers

'I've got this wall,' said my visitor, 'new brickwork and not very pretty. Nineteen and a half feet long. I thought I might plant a clem*a*ytis.'

Clearly, she'd been giving the problem a great deal of attention. Covering the wall was the best solution. Where she went wrong was in assuming that one plant would do it. Two or three climbers would have been better; six, better still – all intermingled. I told her so. Most people can think quite happily about their gardens on the horizontal plane. Good gardeners compose their mixed borders or terraces with imagination giving plenty of thought to colour, texture and everything else that goes into effective planting. But, when it comes to vertical surfaces things don't seem to go quite so well.

Walls, fences, arches, pergolas, upright objects – anything that will carry plant material – are not only parts of the garden that need as much thought over planting as

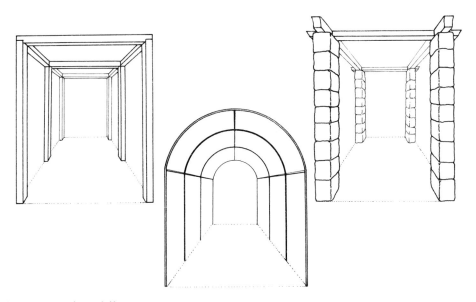

Fig. 29 Pergolas – different types

anywhere else, but are often the key to the rest of the design. In small gardens, especially where there are high boundary dividers to ensure privacy, the area of wall or fence surface may be as big, or even bigger than the ground area. Because liberal gardeners have been open-minded about every other aspect of their gardens, it follows that they will be prepared to try original and exciting ideas for their vertical surfaces. Remembering the preciousness of their time, *laissez-faire* people will not only want to clothe their walls with inspired choices but will expect the wall plants on the whole, to look after themselves. This chapter is designed to help you to achieve such imaginative planting with climbers that will neither swamp your property nor need constant attention.

The vertical garden

Before considering the huge choice of plants that, in nature either climb trees or scramble about on the ground, we should first think about the sites for them in our gardens and about how we can ensure that they will be healthy, happy and undemanding once they are installed.

Sites

Walls are the most obvious sites but there are others. The main point about any wall is that it creates a miniature environment for anything that lives on it or in it. The aspect – north, south, east or west – is important as each carries its own special advantages and disadvantages.

North walls They are often the hardest to furnish but they have the tremendous advantage of constant coolness, less contrast between day and night temperature, and less tendency to dry out. A north wall may be the only source of shade in your garden and will therefore be a valuable site near which to grow your woodland plants.

South walls These are at the opposite extreme. They have the maximum temperature difference between day and night, meaning that tender climbers which begin to emerge prematurely in the early spring sunshine can be hammered by late frost. The ground near a south wall will tend to bake hard – good for Mediterranean irises but bad for climbers that enjoy cool, damp feet. But, a thick south wall retains its heat for some time after sunset and, since they usually look at the sun, flowers on south walls look you right in the eye as you pass.

East walls These will differ profoundly from west walls. They get early morning sun which can be damaging if it shines directly onto frosted foliage. They are also exposed to east winds which, in Europe, are usually the coldest, sometimes driving frost deep into the stonework.

West walls They are more sheltered – west winds are always warmer – and, by the time the sun has got round that far, spring frost should be long gone. Thus, each wall has its own conditions and therefore its own ideal plants.

The nature of the wall will not have much influence on what you can grow up it but porous, crumbly fabric will allow plants to root into it – though this may help to hasten the wall's decay – and though there is probably no difference in actual temperature, mellow brick walls always give the impression of being warmer than grey stone or concrete blocks. Height will not have much influence on what is grown on the wall unless it is so low that the climber must go over the top if it is to be enjoyed at all. Liquid manure sprayed directly onto the wall will encourage plants such as ivies and *Hydrangea petiolaris* to penetrate the masonry and cling more securely with their adventitious roots.

The secret of *laissez-faire* wall gardening is to provide a proper support system. Nails pounded into cracks where they will fit rather than exactly where you wanted them will result in difficulties. Wooden trellis fixed to walls looks fine but only lasts a year or two. Plastic mesh, though I confess to having it here and there, looks unspeakable until it has been covered over completely. The answer is vine eyes – triangular or wedge shaped pieces of galvanised steel with a hole drilled through the thick end. A straight line of vine eyes set into the wall every 6 ft (1.8 m) can be threaded with thick wire which is then held taut and fixed, parallel to the ground, so that it cannot slacken. There should be at least 1 in (2.5 cm) between wire and wall, to make tying-in easier, and the lines of vine eyes should be repeated approximately every 18 in (46 cm) with the lowest about 2 ft (0.6 m) from ground level. If you are building a garden wall from scratch, be sure to install the vine eyes as you go, into the wet cement. In crumbly mortar or where very hard cement has been used, it may be necessary to drill holes with a masonry bit and plug these with wood. The vine eyes or eye bolts can then be screwed into the wood. Going to the bother of equipping a whole wall with climbing wires will save hours of time later on when the plants are established. On crumbly mortar, it may be more sensible to drill the stones or the bricks. Repointing might be necessary if the wall has become badly decayed and vine eyes can be set in as you go, making sure they are securely fixed and that the cement has become thoroughly dry before attempting to stretch the wires through them.

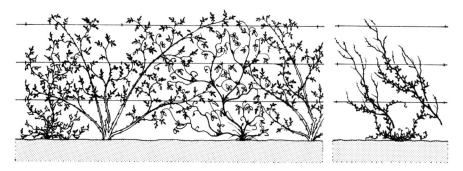

Fig. 30 Walls: interwoven planting; woven peasticks to help new growth

Other structures can be fixed similarly with ties or wires so that routine training of the plants is made as easy as possible. Fences are usually straightforward provided screw-ended vine eyes are used in place of wedge-shaped ones. The weight of a mature creeper is considerable and, once established, it may be necessary to reinforce a fence or wall that has weak posts or crumbling masonry. In extreme cases, rather than using the wall itself as a support, driving posts into the ground adjacent to it and stretching wires regularly between them will not only give the impression that the plants are climbing the wall itself, but will also allow them to benefit from the shelter given by the wall without pulling it down. Thick growths which would be spoilt by excessive thinning can also be reinforced by strong posts set at angles to lean into the structure to prevent collapse. Any unsightly 'legs' sticking out at the bottom will soon disappear under the new growth.

Structures specifically installed for climbing plants can look rather untidy during winter unless well built or well put together. Single posts for pillar roses may be adequate if there is one part of the mixed border where a little narrow height is needed but in isolated spots, they look forlorn in winter. Gazebos and fancy pergolas are usually very expensive and often look more suitable for four days at Chelsea than 30 years in a real garden. The repeated piers of bricks, topped with horizontal beams is the normal 'Homes and Gardens' pergola – not often very convenient for the climbers and nearly as unoriginal as a laburnum tunnel. The two nicest pergolas I have ever seen were 'one off' jobs: the first, consisting of a series of connected mild steel arches led a serpentine route from formal garden into woodland. It had been made by a blacksmith turned agricultural machinery manufacturer who needed a creative outlet to feed his soul after making hundreds of chain harrows. The other was little more than a heavily lichened oak framework – reminiscent of an old timbered building that had lost its tiles and plaster. Planted with *Clematis jackmanii* 'Superba' (purple-blue) and the rose 'Golden Showers' (deep yellow fading to lemon) the grey of the lichened oak made a perfect base colour.

With different levels, sometimes quite big differences, there may be retaining walls. In theory, climbers planted at the tops of these, into the ground, will dangle down, gracefully clothing the walls. In practice, they try to grow upwards, not only spoiling the effect but invading whatever is planted up there. One solution is to grow things *in* the wall – not only little rock plants but larger climbers. Provided their roots can get through into the bank behind the wall they should thrive but, remember, they will also weaken the structure to a certain extent and a sloping bank or wall is safer than a vertical side.

As we have seen with roses (Chapter Seven), trees can make excellent living support for climbers. The same is true of many shrubs – the only precaution being to ensure compatible growth rates. A Russian bindweed planted in a small cherry tree is courting disaster (planting a Russian bindweed anywhere other than on the steppes is imprudent) and expecting a short-stemmed climbing rose to scale a large standard tree is asking too much. Trial and error applies here rather than sticking to book learning because what goes well in one garden will not necessarily repeat itself elsewhere. Certain plants are happier growing out through evergreen cover than anywhere else. For example, *Tropaeolum speciosum* insists on cool roots and a warm head, growing

Fig. 31 Using plants as growing frames: clematis grown on conifer (climbing plant is planted on the north side)

with gusto through yew hedging or rhododendrons to make a stirring splash of crimson when it emerges from the gloomy cover.

Planting the vertical

The owner of a tiny London garden might have a larger area of vertical surface than ground. Clearly, in that case, most gardening time will be spent training and grooming the climbing plants. In larger gardens, although other areas demand much more attention, the vertical surfaces must be made to contribute a great deal. This means that, unless the wall itself is of especial beauty and furnished with occasional plants to set it off, there should be enough material to cover the entire surface. One climber will merge with another so that, once mature, it will be difficult to see any of the brick, concrete block or whatever has been used to build the wall. The choice of plants and how these are arranged will exert an enormous influence on the results. Lack of planning is likely, not only to result in a disappointing display but will also create too much work.

Basic needs

Ground preparation is as vital for wall plants as for anything else. A healthy, thriving climber needs far less attention and will cover the wall more quickly than a plant struggling for survival. Where soil runs up to the base of the wall, planting is easy. Quality can be improved by adding organic material and fertiliser and mulches will improve moisture retention. Where paving or some other hard surface runs right to the wall edge, there is less scope. Planting at intervals into holes knocked through the surface will only work properly if the following are considered:

Holes must be wide and deep enough to accommodate sizeable root systems. You may plant more than one subject in each hole

19. Colchicums used here as foliage plants.
The leaves can become untidy.

20. *Fritillaria meleagris*. The white form of snake's head.

21. *Clematis* 'H.F. Young', a reliable early
bloomer with *Cirsium rivulare*
'Atro-purpureum' in front.

22. The cyclamineus hybrids are good for
    naturalising: 'Peeping Tom' and
    'February Gold'.

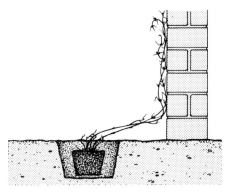

Fig. 32 Planting a clematis to grow up a wall (section)

They must drain adequately

There must be enough of them to house a wide number of plants – one every 10 ft (3.0 m) or so won't do!

They must be capable of receiving adequate rain water – either directly from the sky or indirectly by having the ground sloping towards them – dodgy if the wall happens to be the side of your house!

Because climbers grow so fast and cover such large distances, they usually have large, hungry and thirsty root systems. Planted in the shelter of house eaves, they are unlikely to receive as much water as they need. It may be necessary to plant them up to 3 ft (0.9 m) away from the wall, in extreme cases, but almost always more than a 1 ft (0.3 m).

If the soil is poor and droughty, replace as much as possible with a mix of peat or leaf-mould and good loam. Dressings of slow release fertiliser can be added during planting and should be repeated from time-to-time, particularly when a lot of the climber is to be cut off each year. Thus, pruned clematis and climbing roses will be hungrier for plant food than ivies which are to be left to their own devices. Running around with water will not be part of the *laissez-faire* gardener's working day so it is essential that all new climbers develop good root systems that can seek out water sources below the ground. Thick mulching, as we have seen almost everywhere in the garden, helps to reduce the evaporation rate from the surface of the soil. For certain climbers, mulch is also a necessary protector from direct heat. Honeysuckles and clematis love to flower in full light but dislike warm roots. Several instructional books advise paving slabs over the roots but this is no more effective than a thick layer of leaf-mould or compost. Living mulches – plants that cover and shade the ground – are desirable and add interest. Anything that forms a thick canopy without masking the climbers or competing too strongly with them will do. On hot, south-facing sites, silver-foliaged shrubs like lavenders, santolinas, artemisias or rosemary all have low water requirements but provide pleasant background colour. Elsewhere, the choice is huge but it pays to remember that every plant in the *laissez-faire* garden *must* earn its keep by providing a show itself and must not need solicitous care.

Planning the plants

Since we want our wall garden to be as self-supporting as possible, we must plant carefully. The three categories to use are:

Climbing roses
Skeleton wall plants
Supported creepers and climbers

Roses are in a class of their own because they need more attention than anything else and will represent the lion's share of your routine maintenance work through the year. But, because they contribute so much in terms of colour, scent and interest, they should be a major ingredient of every wall scheme. The variety of different colours, sizes, habits and scents means that there will be a number of good roses to suit practically every mood or style.

Skeleton plants may not be spectacular but will be there to provide a background. Some will be prominent in their seasons but dull for the rest of the year; others, like the ivies, will never shout but will always be there to link the gaps between the high flyers. A skeleton plant must look after itself. Other than an annual check over to trim and anchor any loose bits, it must not only stick up for itself but must provide support, shelter and companionship for the supported creepers and climbers.

Supported creepers and climbers should also, as far as possible, be able to scramble through the skeleton plants or the roses with minimal attention. Some will need cutting hard back once a year, others may get out of control or grow the wrong way and need rescuing. But that should be all. Annual creepers and tender perennial creepers can be added to heighten the attraction provided, once installed, they will not add to the workload.

Summary

1. Vertical surfaces are an essential dimension of any garden

2. The key to trouble-free wall gardening is a proper support system

3. If mortar is weak, drill holes into the brick or stones themselves for the support wires

4. Sprinkle the walls with liquid fertiliser to promote adventitious rooting

5. If considering pergolas think of what the plants will like, not what looks smartest on the glossy magazine page

6. Enrich and mulch ground before planting

7. Plan planting to include skeleton/support plants, creepers to intermingle with these and roses

Planting

Imagine four walls, 6 ft (1.8 m) high and facing north, south, east and west. Plants recommended below are merely ideas and, of course, few walls actually face the four compass points head on. Furthermore, there are other considerations making each site unique. West walls could be exposed; north walls could be sheltered; the positions of buildings, trees and topography will have a profound effect on local conditions. However, the basic planting philosophy should show through this selection so that you can adapt and interpret according to your own special needs.

North wall

Roses Little direct light gets through – so no roses. Vigorous varieties like 'Zéphirine Drouhin' would certainly live on a north wall but would not be very happy and would not flower readily.

Skeleton plants Ivies all thrive in cool shade. The large-leaved forms make thick covers and the coloured-leaf varieties of *Hedera colchica* work well. *H. colchica* 'Variegata' is cream and green but the variety 'Paddy's Pride' has a much more subtle contrast of deep golden green and bottle green streaking. Young, rapidly growing specimens grow enormous leaves which hang in a melancholy fashion. Smaller leaved ivies are easily swamped by *H. colchica* and need siting a distance from it. The silvery-white variegations appeal to me more than the yellow shades but that's a matter of personal taste. Some of the crinkle-leaved ivies and English ivies with odd-shaped leaves are fun to collect although they do not all cling very proficiently. Allow ivies to grow inside support wires. (Wall plants that do not cling directly to the surface of the wall should always be tied to the outsides of the wires to prevent the sawing effect caused by the stems rubbing between wall and wire.) An ivy to avoid is *Hedera canariensis* 'Gloire de Marengo' which is disfigured year after year by frost. The whole point of ivy is its winter foliage. Virgina creepers *(Parthenocissus)* can be useful but many are invasive without contributing much support to anything else. The aristocrat among these plants is *Parthenocissus henryana* because not only are the leaves purplish – a colour that intensifies in the autumn – but they are also marbled with white tracings. Winter jasmine will survive a north wall and the tougher camellias, though they must be pruned and tied in, make wonderful background foliage for summer flowers.

The much vaunted *Hydrangea petiolaris* is constantly recommended for north walls. In its native Japan, it climbs trees but is disinclined to flower in very dark sites. However, in moderate shade a profusion of creamy-white lacecap flowers lights up the area. The beauty of its glossy emerald foliage emerging among the russet stems is almost as stirring as the flower.

Honeysuckles are so good because they will grow wherever their roots are cool. On north walls, where it is excessively dark, they flower less readily than elsewhere but they will certainly thrive. The commonest, *Lonicera periclymenum* 'Belgica' or 'Early Dutch' is one of the best. It seems not to get aphid troubles, flowers uproariously in

May, scrambles everywhere and has a delicious scent. Our wild honeysuckle, especially when the delicate woodbine fragrance blends with wild roses, should not be dismissed. Japanese honeysuckle may not provide a spectacular show but it is evergreen and flowers fragrantly from June to November. It seems equally happy in sun or shade but can become a curse because it roots wherever it touches the ground. Some plant enthusiasts rave about the gold netted version *L. japonica* 'Aureo-reticulata' but this, to me, is a disappointing and sickly looking plant.

Supported climbers and creepers Not many for a truly north wall! The climbing monkshood - *Aconitum volubile* will climb up through the other stuff and produce surprising flowers at head height. In warm counties, the wonderful Chilean *Lapageria rosea* might survive but only on acid soil in complete shelter and warmth. Several clematis are recommended for north walls and some will flower quite well but those that do best are the rampant montana types which are better off climbing into trees. They will flower well if the wall is not too dark and enjoy competing with the honeysuckles. Some *C. alpina* cultivars, especially the paler-coloured or white varieties can be most effective because they flower so early – March in mild years – and have pleasing foliage as well as sporadic secondary blooms from July onwards.

South wall

Roses The number of roses that enjoy being baked up on a hot south wall is limited. Furthermore, the colours are inclined to fade quickly and, in hot weather, the blooms can blow almost as soon as the buds break. However, one or two species relish the warmth and shelter of a hot wall and will mix well enough with other plants. *Rosa banksiae*, usually found as the yellow form *R. b. lutea* loves sun and grows to an immense height producing clusters of cream, double flowers in early summer. Sharp frost will cut it to the ground. The single-flowered yellow 'Mermaid' thrives on heat but is so fiendishly armed that it is best grown where it need not be touched.

Skeleton plants The finest evergreen is undoubtely *Magnolia grandiflora* which, if it never flowered, would still be worth planting for the marvellously glossy foliage. Smaller evergreens like *Carpentaria californica* and *Ceanothus impressus* help to maintain a tropical look which is intensified by woody climbers like *Campsis radicans* and any of the wisterias. *Wisteria sinensis* is deservedly popular but some of the varieties of *W. japonica* especially 'Macrobotrys' and the pink and lilac forms – are well worth growing, even if they take a decade to get bedded in enough to flower impressively. White wisteria has an ethereal beauty not to be missed and by planting several forms, the season can be lengthened. Meanwhile, to while away the years as you await the blooming of the wisterias, more rapid plants can be installed alongside. In warm areas, the passion flowers will produce blooms in late summer. Elsewhere, they just grow leaves but are prolific enough to support other plants.

Chimonanthus praecox is dull in summer, when other climbers can be pleached through it, but in February, when the sweetly-scented blooms come out on sunny days it is the most fragrant plant in the garden. A non-climbing honeysuckle, *Lonicera fragrantissima* can be treated in the same way – as a support in summer but on its own in winter when the tiny white flowers fill the air with sweet scent. Neither of these shrubs climbs and they are best attached loosely to the wall rather than trained in a fan shape. Chimonanthus flowers on old wood, so heavy pruning will do away with some of the flowers. In the pea family, pineapple scented broom, *Cytisus battandieri* and the green stemmed *Piptanthus laburnifolius* both have interesting yellow flowers and excellent foliage. Neither is a habitual wall climber but both are easy to train or half-train onto wall wires. The silver grey foliage of *C. battandieri* makes especially good companion planting for plants with blue, yellow or cream flowers.

Supported climbers and creepers The joy of a hot south wall is that plants will grow up at an astonishing rate so that the resulting jungle of exotic flowers and foliage will make you think winter will never come. Several tender shrubs, particularly the abutilons have good flowers and foliage. The best green leaves are to be found on *Abutilon vitifolium* which also has beautiful mauve-blue flowers. The hybrid *A.* × *suntense* is said to be hardier but not enough to survive with me in eastern England. *Eccremocarpus scaber* seems to be universal these days but is none the worse for that. The tubular orange flowers are quite showy and produced in hundreds. If you're not afraid of sharp yellows, the American native *Fremontodendron californicum* flowers all summer and contrasts well with the blue abutilon, or with blue clematis. As long as their roots are cool and moist, clematis have no objection at all to growing on a south wall but some of the blues and pinks tend to fade. The climbing potato, *Solanum crispum* appeals to some people and loves a south wall but it is ugly out of season.

Though condemned as vulgar by some, the sky-blue saucers of that giant tropical bindweed *Ipomoea tricolor* make the fiddly business of growing it on from seed in the greenhouse worthwhile. Not really a *laissez-faire* plant this, but in a good sunny year, it gives one childish pleasure. The throats of the flowers are not white but primrose. Reminiscent of a pink climbing foxglove, *Maurandia erubescens* will scramble about among the other foliage and flower from late July until frost chops it to the ground. Technically it is a perennial but one should collect seed each year in case the roots are killed off.

East wall

Roses To some, the hardest to furnish but to rose lovers, an east wall poses no problems. There are so many rugged climbers and ramblers that disregard bitter winters and late frost that one is spoilt for choice. The lack of hot, midday sun to scorch blooms is an added benefit and a little burning of the foliage from a May groundfrost is soon healed. It is probably more sensible to mention roses that dislike east walls rather than listing those that grow well. 'Mermaid' and *Rosa banksiae*, have already been mentioned and most of delicate early hybrids like 'Maréchal Niel' are far from hardy but are collectors' items anyway and safer in conservatories. 'Lady Hillingdon' and 'Guinée' both succumbed to a succession of frosts one winter in my Lincolnshire garden but 'Lady Hillingdon' survived from the roots. Other roses seem to love the bracing position.

Skeleton plants The best evergreen for an east wall is *Garrya elliptica*. In full light, twice as many catkins are produced and with an annual pruning to remove stubbornly horizontal branches, it not only looks good itself but makes an excellent clematis support. Several viburnums will grow on an east wall and in a very exposed spot, *V. rhytidophyllum* makes a pleasing green foil for other climbers. Against a wall, the leaves seem to grow larger and stay in better condition than on free-standing plants. The chaenomeles – all of them – love east walls. *C. speciosa* 'Moerloosii' is creamy white turning pink and flowers a little more profusely than the stark white 'Nivalis'. In the *C.* × superba range, 'Crimson & Gold' is a perfect description of the plant and the tritely named 'Pink Lady' warm rose pink with a trace of salmon. The chaenomeles are particularly useful in limy soil which they seem not to mind at all. Though nothing like camellias, they give the winter garden a feeling of chinoiserie. Their summer foliage has nothing to commend it at all but they make good vehicles for clematis.

Supported climbers and creepers East walls are good for clematis, especially those which are cut back every year in early spring. Usually, by the time the young leads are peeping through the foliage of their host plants, the risk of late frost is slight. All the *Clematis viticella* hybrids are good – I can't think of one I dislike – and I have a special soft spot for *C. viticella* 'Alba luxurians'. The faintest trace of blue in the white sepals makes them truly Persil white but their charm lies in the curly green edges to the flowers. There are several other good colours – *C. viticella* 'Rubra' is deep red and 'Minuet' purple fading white to the centres of the flowers. Of the larger-flowered clematis, *C.* × jackmanii is the strongest. There are some good species – all the yellow-flowered clematis from China and Tibet, *C. rehderiana* with its cowslip-scented flowers and *C. macropetala* all enjoy life on an east wall.

West wall

The joy of a west wall is that pretty well everything will thrive on it. There is no early morning sunshine to scorch tender foliage touched with frost, the coldest winds are kept away by the position of the wall and the evening sun shining directly on the wall enables the fabric to store a little heat for the night.

Roses Those inclined to mildew are probably better off in a colder spot but there is barely a rose that would not delight in a warm west wall. Refined climbers of moderate vigour like 'Gloire de Dijon' and 'Spanish Beauty' are especially good.

Skeleton plants Any mentioned above will flourish. In addition, myrtle makes an aromatic choice and the pink flowered *Robinia hispida* is good for summer foliage as well as peaflowers. *Cotoneaster horizontalis* may not be much of a plant itself, although its berries are pleasing in autumn and bees love it in spring, but as a support for clematis and climbers of a more transient nature it takes some beating. Because its stiff branches are held slightly away from the wall, the climbers find it easier to thread themselves through and flower to the front. There are so many good shrubs – hoherias for acid, mild areas, tender jasmines and pittosporums where frosts are few and far between. Pyracanthas come in red, orange and yellow berried forms and there are even species of bramble that are worth growing just for the foliage: *Rubus lineatus* is more or less evergreen with palmate leaves deeply lined on their upper surfaces, and shiny silver beneath. Finally, the more delicate of our buddleias make fragrant plants with good foliage. Easiest of the less hardy species is *B. fallowiana* of which the blue is more likely to survive a bad winter than the white. Usually, even if they have been killed to ground level, buddleias regenerate and flower from nothing in one season.

Supported climbers and creepers Most plants mentioned for the other walls will grow here. To these can be added the large-flowered clematis hybrids, as long as their roots are cool and the golden hop which will contrast well as it scrambles through dark foliage. Perennial sweet peas, *Lathyrus latifolius* are despised because they abound in every cottage garden. But they are common because they are such good garden plants. The white form has a pearly quality and if grown near the normal pinky-purple plants will produce some wonderfully pale offspring. *Lathyrus rotundifolius* carries even more flower than the common everlasting pea and is brick-red.

Summary

1. North walls are coldest but have the most constant temperatures

2. South walls have the greatest temperature extremes. Spring frost is likely to be a problem with them

3. Plants on east walls are susceptible to early morning sun damage after groundfrost

4. West is best. A west wall on a south facing slope – utter bliss for plants and gardeners alike

---

Maintenance

Apart from the roses which will need careful pruning, maintenance should be limited to an annual check over, removing unwanted growth and re-tying. Provided the basic wires are in position, tying-in is not burdensome. Plastic-coated wire is the easiest material to use, making sure the ties are loose enough to allow for secondary thickening in the wood. When pruning wall plants, cut judiciously, making sure you know exactly where the other end is before you snip through what may appear to be a thin stalk. The sight of half the bush quietly keeling over when you've cut through the wrong bit is harrowing. Clematis, except for those species that flower on old wood can be cut hard to the ground, or to just above the lowest couple of buds in March. Large-flowering clematis that get untidy can have the same treatment in early June after flowering. Alternatively, cut them in spring, sacrificing the first flowers to ensure a full season's regeneration.

Annual feeding is important where a lot of material is being cut off. The same fertilising technique as mentioned for roses seems to suit my climbers but the wisterias and evergreen wall shrubs get nothing.

Mice and squirrels can play havoc with young clematis stems, and voles sometimes chew through a main trunk with catastrophic results. The solution is to wind netting round the bottom 10 in (25.4 cm) or to fold a wire mesh over emerging shoots. By the time they are 1 ft (0.3 m) or so long, they seem to lose their sweetness and the rodents leave them alone. Windlash is also a problem with young, tender clematis shoots. Apart from growing them in sheltered conditions there is not much you can do about that. Walls cause particularly vicious eddy currents which can break off young leads. Threading twiggy branches into the wires seems to help without inhibiting the young buds which soon find their way through.

Climbing plants, apart from roses, need little attention and go well in the *laissez-faire* garden. With roses the amount of time you can spare will dictate the number you grow. A rose every 10 ft (3.0 m) interspersed with two or three other climbing plants should result in a fully clad wall – about one plant every 3 ft (0.9 m). Each mature rose takes me, on average, 20 minutes to prune and train. Other wall shrubs average a few minutes each year and species like clematis get done over with shears in a very rough and ready manner. Thus, 100 ft (30.4 m) of wall should not take more than about eight hours per year for everything assuming the wires are sound and stay in position. Planting nothing but ivy and Virginia creeper would eliminate the need to pay the walls any attention at all, but how boring!

CHAPTER NINE

Bulbs for Big Results

The attraction of bulbs is their transience. One moment the ground is bare, the next a flash of colour has arrived from nowhere but, blink and you've missed it. Bulbs contribute enormously while they flower but, apart from daffodils, they have the good grace to exit promptly from the stage as soon as their number has come to an end. Most bulbs flower in spring but there are plenty for other times. Summer brings alliums, agapanthus, ixias, tigridias and gladiolus, and then autumn can be like a second spring with the delicate pinks of nerines, *Amaryllis belladonna,* kaffir lilies and sinister-looking toad lilies. Colchicums appear overnight and the unrelated autumn crocuses – if the mice have overlooked them – can run on to winter, leaving a short Christmas interlude before the snowdrops, aconites and early crocus species start the whole round off again.

Technically, a bulb is a specialised bud with fleshy scale leaves. There are also corms, which are solid rather than composed of scale leaves, tubers, tubercles, rhizomes and so on. Since this is not a text book on botany, we can lump the whole tribe of plants with fleshy storage organs into the general term 'bulbs' without offending anyone other than those pedants whose life's work is to re-name plants on a regular basis so that maximum confusion reigns in horticultural circles. Thus, though not technically bulbous, we shall consider such plants as anemones, cyclamen, schizostylis and so on. Most bulbs are excellent *laissez-faire* plants because:

They need little attention once planted
They provide colour at bad times of the year
They will often flower through ground cover
They are usually invisible when not flowering
Many are easy to multiply
Many naturalise happily
Many belong in the wild garden

Traditionally, bulbs such as large daffodils and Darwin tulips are planted in the herbaceous border where the aftermath of foliage will look untidy until midsummer, or worse, be knotted into hideous loops in the mistaken belief that such torture is beneficial. Smaller species like snowdrops or crocuses are usually called 'rockery bulbs' and get grouped in the most unlikely places – even in motor tyres, filled with soil

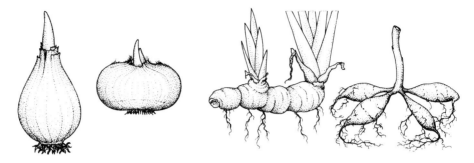

Fig. 33 'Bulb' recognition: *Left to right*: a bulb, a corm, a rhizome, a tuber

and painted white. Since so few new gardeners build rockeries nowadays – not even plum pudding style – it's hard to understand why sales of small bulbs have increased so much lately. Could it be that more people are discovering for themselves the joy of naturalising? Small bulbs can be used to naturalise almost anywhere – in gravel, in mixed borders or in grass – without becoming a nuisance. They do not inhibit plants that follow on and, provided they are happy where they grow, will increase steadily. Larger bulbs need careful siting. Few hybrid tulips naturalise and big daffodils leave a terrible mess behind which must not be cut back if they are to increase. This may be acceptable in grass or under trees but would spoil the June display in a well-managed border. Few bulbs are totally undesirable but, as with all planting, careful thought about where they are to be sited is essential.

Culture

Since bulbs come from such a huge variety of habitats, it is difficult to lay down many hard and fast rules. The *laissez-faire* approach will mean leaving them to their own devices, so as many bulbs as possible must multiply unaided. Bedding out tulips, lifting them after flowering for storage and replanting them elsewhere the following year has no place at all in the *laissez-faire* garden and is more suitable for Parks Departments. However, since some of the large hybrid tulips are so gorgeous, and are so easy to plant, there is no reason why some should not be included in the annual shopping list.

Acquiring the plants

Bulb merchants, like secondhand car salesmen, vary in their ability to supply the right product, in reliable condition at a fair price. A perusal of the popular catalogues will reveal an extraordinary range of prices and some very peculiar naming. Sometimes, the bulbs you receive fail to match up to anything you ordered. The only way to avoid disappointment is to deal with a reliable supplier, preferably one that has been recommended by a fellow gardener or that you know about yourself. Visiting the major spring flower shows, particularly Harrogate and the Royal Horticultural Society shows at Vincent Square, London will enable you to meet and talk to various

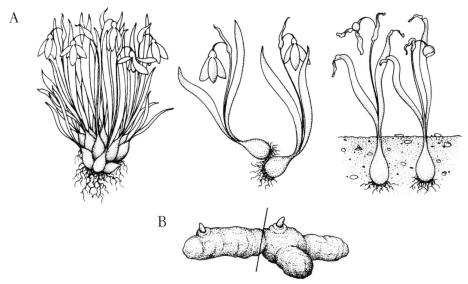

Fig. 34 Bulb division
A Snowdrops: large bulb mass; mass divided; individually planted
B Anemone: rhizome cut, each section having growth bud

bulb people and to see their wares in flower. As you breathe in their delicate perfume and admire their jewel-box colours – of the plants that is, not the suppliers – just remember that some will make better garden subjects than others and that most of what you see at the early shows will have been raised with great care and attention and in some cases, under glass.

These days, an increasing number of bulbs are sold flowering in little pots. The only advantage of this is that you know exactly what you are buying because you can see it there before your eyes in full bloom. Snowdrops and aconites are said to establish better when sold 'in the green' but I am not aware of any trial work carried out to prove or disprove this theory. Certainly, they are easier to handle in the green if, at home, you want to divide the clumps and redistribute. Garden centres usually have display cases of different bulbs from late summer onwards and the choice can be impressive. However, most dedicated bulb enthusiasts prefer to study the merchants' catalogues and purchase by mail order. With the number of firms that specialise in small bulbs these days, the choice of mail order products is so huge and varied that deciding what to buy can be difficult. Unless money is no object, it seems logical to try varieties or species new to your garden in small quantities. Those that like you will do their own multiplying. If they die out, it may not be worth trying them again. Bulbs are far from cheap!

On arrival

Because they are usually delivered dry in October, we tend to forget that bulbs are living plants. After several weeks in brown paper bags or boxes of shavings in the dry atmosphere of a shed or utility room, it is hardly surprising that they deteriorate. Thus, the golden rule is to plant as soon as is practicable. With large tulips, planting can be deferred to ensure later flowering but smaller bulbs, because of their relatively larger surface area, can shrivel with alarming speed. Crocuses, several fritillaries and colchicums sometimes sprout dry, meaning that the fragile shoots are easily broken off on planting. So, as soon as they arrive, get stuck in!

Obviously, not all bulbs are despatched in autumn. Summer flowering plants, especially tender species, will arrive in March or April. The treatment is much the same except that, with the days lengthening and becoming warmer, the rate at which they deteriorate, dry, is faster than in autumn. Tender species can be spoilt by frost but, in Britain, it is unlikely that an April frost will penetrate very deeply into the ground so gladiolus and acidanthera are probably safer planted. With the tender species, a useful trick, if you live in a cold area, is to start them off planted in seed trays with gentle bottom heat. By the time they have emerged and are about 8 in (20 cm) high, frost danger will have passed and they can be planted out. Flowering is brought forward by a month or so this way.

Cyclamen are particularly vulnerable during despatch. They should be planted as soon as they arrive and handled with great care at all times. Cyclamen sold in the growing state, if they have arrived by post, will tend to look horribly mangled but, provided the corms themselves are firm and unblemished, they will recover within a season. Any leaves that have turned yellow must be removed but even healthy foliage will tend to hang off the plant in a sickly fashion once it has been disturbed.

Planting

Different bulbs need different conditions but any special ground preparation is unnecessary. Apart from bedding out, bulb planting is usually a matter of fitting in with other schemes or planting into grass. Just make holes, bung in the bulbs and cover them over. Even upside down, they will right themselves so small nobbly corms or tiny narcissus bulblets do not need careful scrutiny to make sure they are right way up. Larger bulbs are easier to set nose upwards. Planting depth varies with species but the sensible rule seems to be ensure that the nose of the bulb is at least 1 in (2.5 cm) below the surface. Planting tulips deeper helps to prevent them from blowing over but as long as they are buried, precise measurements of depth are not really necessary.

Naturalising

The larger the hybrid, the less natural it looks. Besides using the wrong varieties for naturalising in grass, most people plant very badly. Insensitive persons plant in rows or even in patterns! Next worst are the circle brigade who, mindful of mowing difficulties later, plant neat circles of bulbs 3 ft (1 m) across at regular intervals. Later, they will be doing slaloms between these on their ride-ons. One step up, but still not natural, are the clumpers. Clumpers take a spade and lift divots of turf under which they cram a few bulbs before pushing it back and jumping it down. The resulting clumps congest rapidly and often have different varieties all crammed together.

Horrid! The only way to naturalise properly is to treat each bulb as an individual. Hard work, this, but the rewards are spectacular and what is more, the bulbs multiply well. A useful – well, almost essential – piece of equipment is a bulb planter. If you can't buy one, get one made up by a local lad with a welder.

With the bulb planter, and assuming reasonably short grass, the next job is to distribute the bulbs randomly. The old media gardening experts used to tell us to throw the bulbs about in the naturalising area and to plant them exactly where they fell. For once they were quite right. The bulbs fall singly and in small groups. With the bulb planter, especially if two people can work together, a hole is made wherever there is a bulb, the bulb popped in and the resulting plug replaced, grass uppermost. You'd be amazed at the speed with which planting can progress. One of my daughters and I once got a half hundredweight of daffodils planted in less than an hour and she was only nine at the time! She dropped the bulbs into the holes and replaced the plugs which I trod firmly before coring the next hole. Wherever a single bulb went in there was, six years later, a biggish clump which flowered freely.

Mowing between bulbs will be impossible. In spite of the trial work carried out at Wisley, I have found that daffodils flower better if they are not cut back before the end of June. If the leaves are still green, I sometimes leave them for longer. The grass will look messy for a few weeks but this seems a small price to pay for such lovely spring shows. However, it does mean that care is needed in siting the naturalised area. In large gardens, under trees or in meadow conditions the mess will not irritate but in more confined areas, long, yellowing grass is not likely to elicit murmurs of admiration from the neighbours. One way round the problem is to go for smaller bulbs.

Small bulbs naturalise as readily – often more so – than big daffodils. Often, they die back more quickly after flowering and so the grass can be cut sooner. The choice of colours and variety is wider and, in a small garden, they are less likely to look out of proportion. When planting for naturalisation, the same principle applies as with big bulbs. Scatter them and plant where they fall. There is no need for a bulb planter and, because they are so small, it is not safe to scatter more than a handful at a time, planting

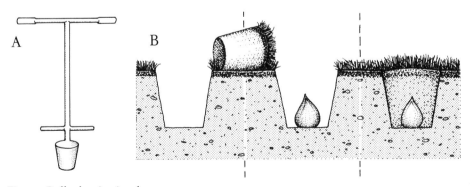

Fig. 35 Bulb planting in a lawn
A Turf hole cutter
B Cut hole; place bulb in hole; replace turf

these before throwing the next lot. The best planting implement is a thin-bladed trowel. Insert this into the turf at an angle of about 45 degrees. Remove the trowel and push the little bulb into the slit. Job done! Snowdrops and aconites can be moved about in the green in this way but their leaves must not be damaged. If they lie on the surface at an odd angle, don't worry. They'll be quite normal next season and, the longer the foliage stays green after transplanting, the better the next flowering will be.

Gravel

The lazy gardener's dream. To plant bulbs, all you do is scrape the surface gravel until you reach the soil or have gone down about 2 in (5.0 cm), lay the bulbs on the ground and scrape the gravel back, smoothing it over. Most small bulbs are so fond of gravel that they seed copiously. This is especially so with scillas and chionodoxas but their seed distribution is very local – seldom more than a yard from the parent plants. To aid distribution, a scoop of gravel taken from here will be impregnated with bulblets and can be scattered about elsewhere on the scree or even spread on soil. The resulting young will flower within a season or two.

Propagation

Bulb nurseries produce interesting new hybrids every year and also introduce new species, some of which become valuable garden plants. It is always worth seeing what they have to offer and most keen gardeners will purchase something new every year. Being an ardent collector, I prefer to buy in variety but, because of economic restraints, am unable to buy anything in very big numbers. Methods of propagating differ with different bulbs but in the *laissez-faire* garden, they should bulk themselves up without too much work input. A surprising number of bulbs, especially small species, reproduce as readily from seed as from bulb division. Most of the tiny narcissi – *Narcissus cyclamineus*, and *N. bulbocodium*, for example, seed freely and, unless their seed thrives, will tend to die out since their bulbs are relatively short lived. Snowdrops seed with gay abandon and introducing some of the larger single-flowered cultivars into your colonies will result in improved strains. Most anemones are easy to raise from seed, either by collecting or sowing or by providing favourable conditions for self-sowing. In gravel, *Anemone fulgens* seeds happily and *A. blanda* will germinate almost anywhere. Larger daffoldils and tulips take years to flower from seed and should be multiplied by division.

In theory, division should take place while the bulbs are dormant – difficult in practice, unless you know precisely where they are. Even then, the chances are, your spade will slice through the middle of the clump. Lifted just after flowering, divided and planted individually, my bulbs seem not to experience any ill effects at all. We are told by eminent horticulturists to do it this way for snowdrops so, why not for daffodils too? If any feeding takes place at all, high potash fertiliser will improve flower size but, for small species and varieties, I dislike the idea of enlarging the flowers unnaturally. Provided the ground is in reasonable heart for the rest of your garden plants, the bulbs will be fine. Whether you want more or not, lifting and dividing clumps will become necessary after some years to prevent the bulbs from becoming increasingly congested and eventually coming blind. Division every other year will result in a high multiplication rate but a single bulb could be left undisturbed for seven years or more before flowering stopped altogether.

Some hybrids or varieties are sterile. The finest *Anemone blanda*, 'White Splendour' refuses to produce seed and must therefore be sliced up. After the top growth has died back, lift the tubers and, with a sharp knife, split them into pieces the size of a peanut shell. Wood anemones *(A. nemorosa)* have worm-like tubers which are easily broken. They should be lifted and replanted after flowering and I have succeeded in doing this before the leaves have died away, splitting them in the same way as a perennial. If you wait for them to die down they are next to impossible to find.

Over-wintering

Tender plants like agapanthus, some gladiolus, *Acidanthera mureliae* and freesias will not survive in the ground outside. True bulbs like agapanthus can be left potted in a cold greenhouse in winter and kept as dry as possible. Corms should be lifted and stored, frost free, in peat which is almost dry but which will not desiccate them. Lifting should be left until all the top growth has turned brown.

Summary

1. Buy from reliable suppliers. Avoid 'bargains' and special offers unless you are sure they are in your interest

2. Some bulbs may transplant better 'in the green'

3. Care for the bulbs as soon as they arrive. Plant as soon as possible or store cool and not too dry – but not soggy

4. Keep tender bulbs frost free over winter

5. Plant bulbs for naturalising at random – not in groups. Invest in a bulb planter for big operations

6. Many small bulbs are short lived and reproduce themselves by seeding. Encourage this by providing the right conditions

---

The choice

This is not a bulb book. The number of different species and varieties of bulbous plants in cultivation is enormous. The object here is to do no more than suggest a few good *laissez-faire* bulbs. The year can be divided into four but we'll leave out the obvious choices, assuming that you already have them or have plans to grow them. We will also look at three typical sites – gravel garden, grass and mixed border.

January to March

Gravel Small crocus species will begin to show now. The *Crocus chrysanthus* varieties are especially charming because of their goblet shapes and bright colours. They are all worthwhile but the cream and white 'Snow Bunting' and 'Zwanenburg Bronze' are especially good. *Crocus ancyrensis* 'Golden Bunch' has egg-yolk flowers which crowd together. For foliage, the gold netted form of *Arum italicum* makes a good gravel plant because the leaves emerge at Christmas time and get larger through the second half of winter.

Grass Snowdrops and aconites will be the mainstay of the winter show naturalised in grass. Besides the common aconite, *Eranthis cilicica* has more feathery leaves which are bronze when they first appear. Among snowdrops, the common *Galanthus nivalis* has many improved forms and the earlier species *G. elwesii* has larger leaves and a very green inner flower. Early daffodils follow on – the two sturdiest N. *Cyclamineus* hybrids being 'February Gold' and 'Peeping Tom,' both of which flower in March. They have swept-back petals and well-formed trumpets.

Mixed border There are more fancy, named snowdrops, such as 'Sam Arnott' and 'Straffan' which are larger than the type and look well in association with hellebores. The spring snowflake *(Leucojum vernum)* begins to flower at 2 in (5.0 cm) but gradually increases its height as the days lengthen. Crown imperials will be on the point of flowering by the end of March, growing up at an astonishing rate on mild days. They smell strongly of fox – unpleasant to most people.

April to June

The climax of the bulb year. Because a high proportion of our garden bulbs are bred from Mediterranean species which have to get their active lives finished before the heat of summer dries the landscape into desert, we are able to enjoy a feast of colour before the main herbaceous shows take over.

Gravel By mid-spring, a bulb lover's gravel garden will be massed with different genera. Anemones – scarlet *Anemone fulgens*, perhaps coloured *A. pavonina* forms ranging from rose-red to deep-blue. Species tulips will be there – multi-headed *Tulipa turkestanica* and the pink and white lady tulip *T. clusiana*. One or two small narcissi love gravel: *N. juncifolius* is a tiny buttercup-yellow affair but the flowers are so perfectly formed – like tiny jonquils. Jonquils *(N. jonquilla)* themselves tend to flower later and have marvellous scent. Antiquarian gardeners will have the beautiful double form – 'Queen Anne's Double' which goes back to before 1700.

But the most interesting plants are the fritillaries – not just snakesheads which are better in grass but any of the hundreds of drooping bell flowers coloured brown, yellow, green and shades in between. Some multiply well in gravel. *Fritillaria graeca, F. pyrenaica* and *F. persica* are among the easiest.

23. The rugosa hybrid 'Mrs Anthony Waterer'. Superb scent, good disease resistance.

24. *Papaver orientale* 'Goliath'. The reddest of all big poppies.

Grass (naturalised) Anything that can slog it out with grasses, cowslips, campion, cowparsley, kingcups, buttercups or whatever else you have managed to establish in the grass deserves its place. On a big scale the modern daffodils will create a good spring show. In more refined areas where species such as snakesheads *(Fritillaria meleagris)*, dog's tooth violet and bluebells are used, care must be taken not to spoil the proportions by introducing anything too large and showy. Plants that inhabit woodland floors from any part of the temperate world will usually grow well together but once their hybrids are introduced, care is needed. *Anemone pavonina*, for example, will naturalise well alongside such species as *Fritillaria meleagris* but big florists' anemones will not. Pot hyacinths, planted outside, are more attractive after a few years when they have degenerated to produce half-a-dozen small stems, each carrying a handful of blooms than when the enlarged bulbs threw up a single blob of colour with as much appeal as a spear of broccoli.

Mixed border More fritillaries: the crown imperials familiar to everyone and, for damp soil, a superb brooding black species from North America – *Fritillaria camschatcensis* – which flowers in early June. The last tulip to flower, *T. sprengeri* multiplies well from self-sown seed and has startling scarlet flowers with straw-coloured petal backs in late May. Of all species tulips it is the loveliest and one of the easiest to grow. Why is it so uncommon in gardens?

A friend of mine buys a few smart modern tulip hybrids each year. He plants strictly to colour but quite informally, thrusting the bulbs in where they will fit in his crowded cottage garden. Part of his front garden is devoted to lavender, cream and white plants with strayings to pink here and there. He allows ox eye daisies *(Chrysanthemum leucanthemum)* and red campion *(Silene dioica)* to stray among these queens of Chelsea and very pretty it all looks too. One must not be snobbish about plants.

July to September

Gravel The garlics are useful here as well as in the mixed border. Two particular little beauties are *Allium senescens* which has a mass of small pink heads over a forest of dense, neat foliage and a beautiful blue species *A. cyaneum* which never gets more than 6 in (15.2 cm) high and has grassy foliage. Some of the South African bulbs are fun in gravel. The gorgeous lilac mauve inflorescences of *Tulbaghia violacea* come in regular flushes from midsummer onwards. Any thoughts of picking a bunch for the house must be banished from the mind for it smells worse than the foetid exhalation of a perished rubber inner-tube. Tulbaghias need winter protection. For late summer scent, the gladiolus relative *Acidanthera mureliae* is essential planting. The nodding white flowers have deep purple blue eyes.

Grass A dull time for bulbs in grass. Scars from the Big Cut Back take a few weeks to disappear.

Mixed border The late gladiolus *Gladiolus papilio* makes a perfect end to the quarter which will have livened up earlier on with large, white *Galtonia candicans* – a perfect *laissez-faire* plant because it multiplies so easily from seed. Eremurus are fun to grow.

Eremurus bungei produces foxtails of mid-yellow flowers but the spectacular species is the huge, priapic *Eremurus robustus* which soars to 8 ft (2.4 m) in the right conditions and elicits comment from every passer-by!

Lilies are perfect for mixed borders but on limy soils, few species thrive and multiply. Exceptions are tiger lilies (*Lilium tigrinum*) with their hybrids and the enormous *L. henryi*, whose tangerine flowers come out in August at a height of at least 6 ft (1.8 m). Lilies are greedy feeders, loving thick mulches and roots shaded by neighbouring shrubs.

October to December

Gravel Crocus time again. The autumn species are happy in gravel but mice and voles love to dig up the corms and eat them just as they are about to flower. *C. speciosus* is the prettiest but in large numbers, the frail little cream *C. ochroleucus* can be interesting because it flowers in November. There is an attractive autumn flowering snowflake *(Leucojum autumnale)* – very small, pink-tinged white flowers but pleasant enough. There are even two autumn flowering snowdrops. The literature states that *Galanthus corcyrensis* is synonymous with *G. nivalis* subspecies *reginae olgae* but in my garden I have two autumn snowdrops, one flowering in September, the other in November. They are quite different in appearance and habit and, according to my labelling, the later flowering plant is *G. corcyrensis*.

Schizostylis coccinea enjoys the sharp drainage of gravel. To make it flower profusely it must be lifted and split every few years but on gravel it spreads so well you may have to exert a touch of discipline! There are several good varieties in various shades of pink, newest of which is 'Jennifer' – a pale sport of *S. coccinea* 'Major'.

Grass Colchicums grow wild in European meadows. Naturalised among grass, their autumn flowers show well and the ugliness of their spring foliage is diluted among the other vegetation. *Crocus speciosus* naturalises as well in short grass as in gravel.

Mixed borders The nerines will need a warm, peaty, acid or neutral soil to flower well but, when they like you, they produce a succession of pink umbels which are as good in the garden as picked for the house. *Amaryllis belladonna* is less easy but so beautiful it is worth a try. The leafless stems are quite dark but when the flowers open they are soft-pink – the colour of strawberry ice-cream. In warm areas, yellow crocus-like blooms of *Sternbergia lutea* come out in late October but it is an ill-natured plant, sulking in most gardens and refusing to multiply.

Having developed a taste for interesting bulbs, you will need to negotiate a pay rise because many of the unusual species are expensive to buy. However, there is never any hurry in gardening and a few additions each year will be plenty to keep you going, even if this year's introductions take several seasons to multiply enough to provide a reasonable display. If you haven't already done it, a trip to the Mediterranean in April will get you well and truly hooked. All the temporarily green meadows and even the roadside verges twinkle with asphodels, narcissus, scarlet anemones, grape hyacinths and a myriad tiny irises. If sights like that don't move you, throw this book away at once and take up a different hobby. How about folk dancing?

CHAPTER TEN

Laissez-faire Lawns

That this is the shortest chapter says a lot for the importance I place on lawn care. That there is a chapter on lawns at all shows that they do have some importance. There is often thought to be something not quite nice about a gardener who does not look after his lawns with solicitous care. Is it not somewhat un-British to have daisies growing there, or to have untidy edges? The conscientious lawn man – it's almost always a man! – spends an amazing amount of time aerating, feeding, rolling, mowing, weedkilling and scarifying his emerald patch. Of course, it provides wonderful opportunities for the gadget gardener. There are patent whizzlers, whirrers, sprinklers, scarifiers, applicators and even a kind of running spike which you strap onto your shoe and hop about thus aerating the ground and exercising your body at the same time!

Lawn fanatics and *laissez-faire* gardeners do not make happy companions. The keen lawn groomer will not have time to do any real gardening and will probably take exception to the 'laid back' approach. However, grass is an essential part of most gardens – with the exception of tiny town plots where stone paving or gravel makes far more sense – and a minimum of management is necessary. Badly-managed grass will wear out quickly, will go brown too soon in droughty weather and, in extreme cases, can spoil the whole garden. Proof of this becomes apparent when you see the transformation that occurs when you have just mown your grass. Weedy borders don't look half so bad when they are separated by short lawns with neatly trimmed edges.

Maintenance

Lawns suffer from a variety of complaints and we will look briefly at those commonly experienced:

Wear and tear

The type of grass grown does matter. Heavy wear needs heavy-duty grass. These days, seedsmen offer a wide range of mixtures and will advise on special blends for different purposes. Going for expensive mixes made with the finest-leaved species may be ideal for bowling greens but would not be necessary in a *laissez-faire* garden. Using an inexpensive mix, with ryegrass, results in a serviceable sward which will stand up to heavy use. I haven't mentioned turf, as opposed to sowing grass seed, because I have always found seed to be cheaper, easier and almost as quick to establish a healthy sward. I have never understood the reason for buying turves. Instant gardening I suppose!

At trouble spots – where paths join lawns or on well-trod corners, laying paving slabs into the grass will prevent mud patches from developing. To avoid mower damage, they must be let in so that the turf is proud of the stone. The edges of the turf will mould down over them and only need be trimmed at the edge once a year.

Weeds

The obsessive lawn groomer will use weedkiller at least once a year and is likely to back up his spring onslaught with a supplementary treatment or two during the summer. *Laissez-faire* lawns need not suffer this much attention but, unless steps are taken to control the worst weeds, eventually they will take over and ruin the sward. (Sward, in this instance, means vegetative cover – it doesn't have to be 100 per cent grass but there should be more grass than anything else.) If daisies, plantains, yarrow or clover are becoming too plentiful, a single treatment of proprietary weed/feed mix in April should cope with the problem by allowing the grass to regain its supremacy. Be sure to comply with the instructions on the bag.

This action is only necessary when weeds have become a major problem and need not be repeated every year. Organic gardeners will have to rely on management. This means not cutting the grass too short and preventing any of the lawn weeds from seeding. If the non-grass plants in the lawn are welcome – as they frequently are among conservation-minded gardeners these days, the entire regime must be completely different but what is being grown in this case is not a lawn but a meadow. Meadows belong in wild areas and, if sited where a lawn should be, may well spoil the design of your garden.

Starvation

Grass is a glutton for nitrogen; if it is in short supply, the grass looks yellow and the chances of weeds spreading at the expense of the grass is increased. An annual treatment of nitrogen fertiliser is enough for non-organic gardeners and is most easily applied with the weedkiller as a weed/feed mix described above. However, if weeding is unnecessary, ammonium nitrate granules can be broadcast, preferably in damp weather, at a rate of roughly 1 oz per sq yd (30 g per sq m). Since the response of grass to nitrogen is almost unlimited, perfect accuracy is not essential but uneven distribution will result in patchiness. An autumn feed containing phosphorus and potash will benefit the grass too but is by no means essential.

Organic lawn groomers must rely on the natural cycle – always remembering that lawns are far from natural – and cut less frequently, leaving the grass mowings on the surface from time to time when weather ensures that they will dry and disappear rapidly.

Disease

The *laissez-faire* lawn is not likely to become diseased unless cut too short, too frequently. With adequate feeding and allowing the grass to exist at a reasonable length – at least 1 in (2.5 cm) in the most manicured areas, longer elswhere – the grass should be able to outgrow any fungal problems.

Moss

However well drained and well managed they are, most lawns grow moss at some time or other. This is usually squeezed out by the grass once the season gets under way. Treatments of iron-sulphate blacken moss impressively but if this is not raked out quickly it recovers until the grass is able to compete with it. Grass grows far better on well-drained soil and therefore is more likely to suppress the moss. In dense shade, moss may be the only green stuff that will grow!

Drought

The choice is simple: water in times of drought, or put up with brown lawns. They always recover as soon as the rain comes. The effect of drought can be delayed by not mowing closely and now that rotary mowers do such an excellent job, it is possible to have smooth, even grass without having to scalp it. Rotary mowers with back rollers, rather than wheels, produce a striped effect so there really is nothing to gain from using a cylinder machine. Healthy grass in well-drained conditions stays green longer in dry weather because the root systems go deeper. If the lawn is already established, the various methods of draining usually recommended – all basically consisting of making holes at intervals – are easier to read about than to do. Earthworms assist with their little burrows and are highly desirable in a balanced lawn, despite the casts which are a minimal nuisance. If a new lawn is to be laid, be sure to get the drainage right first. (See Chapter Three.)

Edges

'Doing the edges' is a hellish chore which dates back to the days of apprentice gardeners and surplus labour. Any well-designed garden must have dividing lines between lawn and border. It simply isn't feasible to merge one imperceptibly into the other. Long handled shears are the only tools that will trim conventional lawn edges. Nothing, absolutely nothing else works. No, really it doesn't! Stone or concrete (concealed) edging can reduce the work involved and laying a pathway flush – or even slightly lower than the grass will be hard work to install but will save hundreds of hours of heavy work.

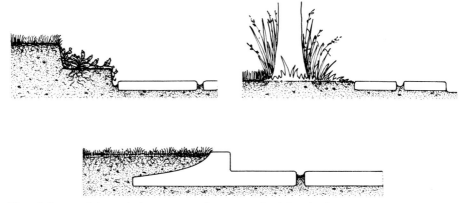

Fig. 36 Lawn-edging techniques: ground cover; path edging; kerb

Where grass is grown long, for example after bulbs or as a wild meadow, mowing paths through it and keeping a band – say 3 ft (0.9 m) in width – close mown round the edges will enhance the appearance, making the meadow look as though it is intended rather than a result of neglect. Close-mown rides down long avenues of trees with long grass at their feet pleases the eye and serves a useful practical purpose into the bargain.

Meadows

So many theoreticians exhort us to have meadows rather than lawns these days. Often, such people live in neat suburban villas and reach for the 2,4-D when nobody's looking. Meadows are possible to manage on a small scale but are much easier where there is room. The basic rules are not to feed and to know when to cut.

Grass that is never cut eventually transforms into forest. Grass cut too frequently never grows flowers. All the wild perennials die leaving nothing behind but a limited range of grasses. Most 'natural' meadows reach the annual climax of growth a week or two after the longest day. A heavy cut in late July therefore enables the wild plants to seed. A second cut in October ensures a short sward for the spring show. Further cuts throughout the autumn may help to keep the grass from growing too coarse but are not essential.

As long as no fertiliser goes near it and as long as all the mowings are removed every time, the soil should become impoverished enough for the shorter grasses to dominate the sward and allow meadow flora to flourish – the poorer the soil, the better the flowers. When the grass is reasonably thin, establishing meadow plants is easier. (See Chapter Four.)

Although grass plays a vital role in garden design, *laissez-faire* gardeners will find life easiest if they are able to compromise between total neglect and over-conscientious care of their lawns. An annual feed and weed and judicious cutting at a reasonable length will usually be enough, assuming reasonable drainage and robust grasses.

Installing some of the devices mentioned to reduce the chore of edging will help too. A filthy, unhealthy lawn can ruin an otherwise well-run garden, but the faultless emerald rectangle might make people feel a little uncomfortable – especially if no one is allowed to set foot on it.

That brings us to the end of this book. The aim has been to inspire you with a few ideas. Probably, you knew much of the content before but, if it has helped to show that one can be a keen and competent gardener while pursuing a busy career *and* indulge in other hobbies at the same time, then its objective has been achieved. There is no need for the world to disappear under a sea of heather, conifers and artificial stone paving! We must cast off the shackles of earlier constraints without losing sight of the superb artistry of our gardening forebears. We must approach today's garden problems with an open and versatile mind but, above all, whatever motivates us, our gardening must be something we enjoy – it must be fun!

Plant List

Plants mentioned in the text are listed below together with several additions. The list is not intended to be comprehensive but was devised to give you a few ideas. Some plants are easier to grow than others and for guidance, the following information is included with each entry:

Name The scientific name is written first, followed by an English colloquial name where appropriate.

LFG rate This is an attempt to rate the item according to its suitability as a *laissez-faire* plant. The evaluation is subjective but based on garden worthiness – i.e. beauty – ease of propagation, resistance to disease and lack of troublesome invasiveness. A *** plant will look beautiful for a long season, will reproduce itself without help, often has more than one attribute such as foliage plus flower, or winter twigs plus summer foliage and is unlikely to become a nuisance. A * plant will have certain disadvantages – such as needing careful propagation or being subject to late frost damage – but is still a worthwhile plant which will perform well without too much work input. A ** plant is somewhere between the two.

Type
>   A = Hardy annual
>   AH = Alpine plant suitable for scree or rock garden
>   B = Bulb (corm, rhizome, tuber etc)
>   CH = Climbing herbaceous
>   CW = Climbing woody plant
>   H = Herbaceous plant of any size (not alpines but down to small perennials)
>   (T) = Tender plant
>   W = Woody i.e. a shrub or tree

Height Given in cm. GC = Ground cover (20 cm or less where no height given).

Aspect Plant's preferred aspect – S = sun or Sh = shade.

Conditions Wet, dry, moist, (med = midway between, not too wet but not baking dry). ° = limehater.

Season Sp = late Mar to June. Su = June to Sept. Au = Oct to Dec. Wi = Jan to March. Con = year-round interest.

Effect The chief reasons for growing the plant – Fl = flowers. Fr = fruit. Fo = foliage. St = stems or winter twigs.

Colour Main colour given plus any relevant information.

Plant name	LFG rate	Type	Hght/cms	Aspect	Conditions	Effect	Season	Colour
Abutilon vitifolium	*	W(T)	200+	S	Med	Fl/Fo	Su	Blue/big leaves
Abutilon × suntense	**	CW	200+	S	Med	Fl/Fo	Su	Mauve
Acaena caerulea	**	H	GC	S	Any	Fo	Con	Glaucous foliage
A. 'Copper Carpet'	*	H	GC	S	Dry	Fo	Con	Khaki foliage
Acanthus mollis	**	H	90	S/Sh	Med	Fl/Fo	Su/Au	Pink and green flowers
A. Spinosus	**	H	90	S/Sh	Med	Fl/Fo	Su/Au	Pink, green, spiky
Acer campestre, Field Maple	*	W	1500	S	Any	Fo	Con	Autumn colour
A. griseum	**	W	450	Sh	Med	Fo/St	Con	Sloughing bark
A. palmatum cultivars	**	W	100+	S/Sh	Med°	Fo/St	Con	Leaf colours
Acidanthera mureliae	*	B(T)	60	S	Med	Fl	Su/Au	White-blue eyes
Aconitum anglicum, Monkshood	***	H	60	S/Sh	Any	Fl	Sp/Su	Blue
A. × arendsii	***	H	120	S/Sh	Moist	Fl	Au	Deep blue
A. 'Ivorine'	**	H	90	Sh	Med	Fl	Sp/Su	Cream
A. napellus	***	H	75	S	Med	Fl	Su	Deep blue
A. volubile, Climbing monkshood	*	CH	180	Sh	Med	Fl	Su	Blue
Ajuga pyramidalis	**	H	GC	Sh	Moist	Fl/Fo	Con	Blue
A. reptans cultivars	***	H	GC	Sh/S	Moist	Fo/Fl	Con	Bronze/pink foliage
Alchemilla alpina	*	AH	15	S	Dry	Fo	Sp/Su	Green
A. conjuncta	**	H	15	S	Dry	Fo/Fl	Sp/Su	Silverbacked green
A. mollis, Lady's Mantle	*	H	30	S/Sh	Any	Fo/Fl	Con	Green invasive
Allium cyaneum	**	B	15	S	Dry	Fl	Su	Blue

Plant name	LFG rate	Type	Hght/cms	Aspect	Conditions	Effect	Season	Colour
Allium giganteum	**	B	120	S	Med	Fl	Su	Large, purple
A. moly	*	B	20	S	Any	Fl	Sp	Yellow, invasive
A. senescens	***	B	20	S	Med	Fl/Fo	Su	Plummy pink
A. siculum	***	B	75	S	Med	Fl	Su	Pinkish
A. sphaeracephalum	**	B	45	S	Dry	Fl	Su	Dark wine red
Amaryllis belladonna	*	B	45	S	Dry	Fl	Au	Pink
Althaea rosea, Hollyhock	**	H	250	S	Dry	Fl	Su	Pink/red/yellow
A. rugosa	***	H	150	S	Dry	Fl	Su	Lemon yellow
Anemone blanda	***	B	10	S	Dry	Fl	Sp	Blue
A. b. 'White Splendour'	**	B	15	S	Dry	Fl	Sp	White
A. fulgens	***	B	20	S	Med	Fl	Sp	Scarlet
A. hupehensis hybrids	***	H	75	S/Sh	Any	Fl	Su/Au	Pink/white
A. magellanica	*	H	20	Sh	Med	Fl	Sp	Creamy white
A. nemorosa, Wood anemone	***	H	20	Sh	Med	Fl	Sp	White
A. n. Robinsoniana	***	H	20	Sh	Med	Fl	Sp	Lilac blue
A. pavonina cultivars	***	B	15	S	Dry	Fl	Sp	Blue/pink/mauve
Anthemis cupaniana	*	H	20	S	Dry	Fl/Fo	Con	Silver foliage/White flowers
Anthriscus sylvestris, Cow parsley	*	H	75	Sh	Any	Fl	Sp/Su	White, invasive
Aquilegia alpina	***	H	30	S/Sh	Med	Fl	Sp/Su	Blue
A. viridiflora	*	AH	20	S	Med	Fl	Sp	Brown and green
A. vulgaris cultivars	***	H	45+	S/Sh	Med	Fl	Sp/Su	Pink/blue/white
Arabis caucasica 'Flora-pleno'	***	AH	20	S	Any	Fl	Sp	White
A. ferdinandi-coburgii 'variegata'	**	AH	5	S	Any	Fo	Con	Green/cream foliage
Arisarum proboscideum	***	H	15	Sh	Moist	Fl	Sp	Spathes like mice
Arum italicum 'pictum'	***	H	30	Sh/Su	Any	Fo	Wi/Sp	Gold netted leaves
A. maculatum	*	H	30	Sh	Med	Fo	Sp	Green
Artemisia absinthium	*	H	60	S	Dry	Fo	Con	Silver green
A. 'Powis Castle'	*	W	60	S	Dry	Fo	Con	Silver filigree
Aruncus dioicus	***	H	120	Sh	Med	Fl/Fo	Sp/Su	Creamy plumes
Arundinaria viridistriata	*	W	90	S	Any	Fo	Con	Gold/green stripes
Asphodeline liburnica	**	H	90	S	Med	Fl	Su	Pale yellow

Plant name	LFG rate	Type	Hght/cms	Aspect	Conditions	Effect	Season	Colour
A. lutea	**	H	100	S	Med	Fl	Su	Sharp yellow
Asplenium trichomanes	**	AH	10	Sh	Dry	Fo	Con	Wall fern
Aster amellus 'King George'	*	H	45	S	Any	Fl	Au	Blue
A. capensis 'Santa Anita'	*	T	45	S	Dry	Fl	Su	Bright blue
A. novi angliae cultivars	**	H	90	S	Any	Fl	Au	Red/pink/white
Astrantia major and cultivars	***	H	60	S	Med	Fl	Su	Pink/white/green
A. maxima	***	H	60	S/Sh	Med	Fl	Su	Pink
Aubrietia hybrids	**	AH	10	S	Dry	Fl	Sp	Mauve shades
Bergenia cultivars	*	H	30	S/Sh	Dry	Fo/Fl	Sp	Pink/white/purple
Betula nana, Dwarf birch	*	W	45	S/Sh	Any	Fo	Sp/Su	Green foliage
Brunnera macrophylla & cultivars	***	H	60	Sh	Med	Fl/Fo	Sp/Su	Blue/big leaf
Buddleia davidii	**	W	300+	S	Dry	Fl	Su	Blue/purple/white
B. fallowiana	**	W(T)	180	S	Dry	Fl/Fo	Su	Mauve/white
Butomus umbellatus, flowering rush	*	H	75	S	Moist	Fl	Su	Pink
Caltha palustris, Kingcups	***	H	30	S	Wet	Fl	Sp	Golden yellow
Campanula rotundifolia, Harebell	**	H	20	S	Dry	Fl	Su	Blue Wildflower
Carex buchananii	*	H	60	S	Any	Fo	Con	Tan sedge
C. Pendula, Pendulous sedge	*	H	90	Sh	Moist	Fo	Con	Pendulous flowers
Campsis radicans	**	CW	400	S	Dry	Fl	Su	Red/orange
Cardamine pratensis, Cuckoo flower	***	H	20	S	Moist	Fl	Sp	Lilac foodplant
Carpentaria californica	*	W	150	S	Dry	Fl	Su	White, evergreen
Carpinus betula, Hornbeam	***	W	1800+	S/Sh	Any	Fo	Con	Hedging, etc.
Catananche coerulea	**	H	45	S	Dry	Fl	Su	Blue
Ceanothus impressus cultivars	**	W(T)	240	S	Med	Fl/Fo	Su	Blue shades
Ceterach officinarum	*	AH	10	Sh	Dry	Fo	Cont	Wall plant
Centaurea cyanus, Cornflower	***	A	45	S	Dry	Fl	Su	Peacock blue
C. montana	*	H	45	S	Med	Fl	Su	Blue/white
C. nigra, Hardheads	*	H	45	S	Med	Fl	Su	Rose red
C. scabiosa, Greater Knapweed	*	H	60	S	Dry	Fl	Su	Rose red
Centranthus ruber	**	H	60	S	Dry	Fl	Su	Pink/coral/white

Plant name	LFG rate	Type	Hght/cms	Aspect	Conditions	Effect	Season	Colour
Chaenomeles speciosa 'Moerloosii'	***	W	180	S	Any	Fl	Wi/Sp	White fading pink
C. s. 'Nivalis'	***	W	180	S	Any	Fl	Wi/Sp	Pure white
C. × superba 'Crimson and Gold'	***	W	160	S	Any	Fl	Wi/Sp	Crimson
C. × s. 'Pink Lady'	***	W	160	S	Any	Fl	Wi/Sp	Mid pink
Chaerophyllum hirsutum roseum	***	H	60	Sh	Moist	Fl/Fo	Sp/Su	Lacy pink
Chamaecyparis 'Green Globe'	**	W	30	S	Any	Fo	Con	Dwarf conifer
Chamaespartium saggitale	***	AH	15	S	Dry	Fl	Su	Yellow, spreader
Chrysanthemum leucanthemum, Moon Daisy	*	H	60	S	Any	Fl	Su	White, invasive
C. segetum, Corn Marigold	*	H	45	S	Any	Fl	Su	Yellow, invasive
C. uliginosum, Jumpers	***	H	180	S	Moist	Fl	Su/Au	Tall white daisy
Chrysoplenum davidianum	**	AH	10	Sh	Moist	Fl	Sp	Golden green
Cimicifuga simplex	***	H	120	Sh	Moist	Fl	Au	White plumy flowers
Clarkia elegans	*	A	45	S	Med	Fl	Su	Red/pink shades
Clematis alpina cultivars	***	CW	—	S/Sh	Med	Fl	Sp/Au	Blue/pink/white
C. macropetala cultivars	***	CW	—	S/Sh	Med	Fl	Sp	Blue/pink/white
C. × durandii	***	H	180	S/Sh	Med	Fl	Su	Rich blue, satiny
C. heracleifolia davidiana	*	H	100	S/Sh	Med	Fl	Su/Au	Blue scented
C. integrifolia	***	H	90	S/Sh	Med	Fl	Su	Blue
C. × jackmanii	***	CW	—	S/Sh	Med	Fl	Su/Au	Royal blue
C. × jouiniana	***	H	90	S/Sh	Med	Fl	Au	Off white-blue
C. orientalis	***	CW	—	S/Sh	Med	Fl/Fr	Su/Au	Yellow
C. rehderiana	**	CW	—	S	Med	Fl	Su	Straw, scent
C. tangutica	***	CW	—	S/Sh	Med	Fl/Fr	Su/Au	Yellow/seedheads
C. viticella cultivars	***	CW	240+	S/Sh	Med	Fl	Su	Blue/red/white
Colchicum autumnale, Meadow Saffron	**	B	10	S	Med	Fl	Au	Pinkish mauve
C. byzantinum	***	B	15	S	Med	Fl	Au	Lilac mauve
C. speciosum	**	B	15	S	Med	Fl	Au	Lilac mauve/white
C. sp. 'Waterlily'	*	B	15	S	Med	Fl	Au	Double flower
Cornus alba cultivars	*	W	180+	S	Moist	St/Fo	Wi	Coloured twigs
C. mas	**	W	250+	S/Sh	Any	Fl/Fo	Wi/Au	Yellow flowers

Plant name	LFG rate	Type	Hght/cms	Aspect	Conditions	Effect	Season	Colour
Cosmos atrosanguineus	*	H(T)	45	S	Med	Fl	Su	Chocolate maroon
Cotoneaster dammeri 'radicans'	***	W	GC	S	Med	Fo	Su	Berries
C. horizontalis	***	CW	240	S	Any	Fo/Fr	Con	Red berries
Crambe cordifolia	***	H	250	S	Med	Fl/Fo	Su	Big leaf/white flowers
Crataegus monogyna cultivars	*	W	360+	S/Sh	Any	Fl/Fr	Sp/Au	White/pink/red
Crocosmia cultivars	**	B	60+	S	Dry	Fl	Su/Au	Orange/red/yellow
Crocus ancyrensis 'Golden Bunch'	***	B	6	S	Dry	Fl	Wi/Sp	Eggyolk yellow
C. imperatii	***	B	6	S	Dry	Fl	Wi	Buff, blue
C. speciosus	***	B	10	S	Dry	Fl	Au	Bluish purple
C. chrysanthus cultivars	***	B	7	S	Dry	Fl	Wi/Sp	Yellow/white/purple
Cyclamen coum	***	AH	10	S	Dry	Fl/Fo	Wi	Pink/white
C. cilicium	**	AH	10	S	Dry	Fl/Fo	Au	Pale pink
C. hederifolium	***	H	15	S/Sh	Med	Fl/Fo	Au	Pink/white
C. purpurascens	*	H	15	Sh	Med	Fl	Su	Purple pink
C. repandum	*	H	10	Sh	Med	Fl	Sp	Deep pink
Cytisus battandieri	**	W	300	S	Dry	Fl/Fo	Su	Yellow, scent
C. decumbens	***	AH	10	S	Dry	Fl	Sp	Yellow, spreader
C. praecox	*	W	150	S	Dry	Fl	Sp	Pale yellow
Daphne blagayana	*	W	100	Sh	Moist	Fl	Sp	Cream, fragrant
D. × burkwoodii	**	W	90	S	Med	Fl	Sp	Pale pink
D. cneorum 'Eximea'	***	W	25	S	Med	Fl	Sp	Pink
D. collina	**	W	45	S	Med	Fl/Fo	Sp	Pink, evergreen
D. odora	*	W	75	Sh	Med°	Fl/Fo	Sp	Pink, evergreen
Dentaria digitata	**	H	30	Sh	Med	Fl	Sp	Lilac mauve
D. enneaphylla	***	H	30	Sh	Med	Fl	Sp	Cream
Dianthus deltoides	**	AH	15	S	Dry	Fl	Su	Wine red
Dianthus Hybrids – Alpine pinks	***	AH	15	S	Dry	Fl/Fo	Su	Pink/red/white
– 'Pike's Pink'	***	AH	10	S	Dry	Fl	Su	Clear pink
Dianthus Hybrids – Old pinks	***	H	25	S	Dry	Fl	Su	Pink/red/white
Digitalis ambigua	*	H	45	Sh	Dry	Fl	Su	Cream and rust
D. ferruginea	**	H	75	Sh	Dry	Fl	Su	Rusty cream
D. lutea	**	H	75	Sh	Med	Fl	Su	Lemon

Plant name	LFG rate	Type	Hght/cms	Aspect	Conditions	Effect	Season	Colour
Digitalis purpurea, Foxglove	***	H	100	Sh	Med	Fl	Su	Purple/white/pink
Dicentra eximia	***	H	30	S	Med	Fl/Fo	Sp/Su	Pink/ferny foliage
D. formosa cultivars	***	H	30+	S	Med	Fo/Fl	Sp/Su	Pink/red/white
Doronicum caucasicum, Leopardsbane	**	H	30+	S	Med	Fl	Sp	Yellow
Eccremocarpus scaber	**	CH	180	S	Med	Fl	Su/Au	Orange
Echinops ritro	*	H	120	S	Med	Fl	Su	Blue
Elaeagnus pungens 'Maculata'	*	W	150	S/Sh	Med	Fo	Con	Cream/yellow foliage
E. × ebbingei 'Limelight'	**	W	150	S	Med	Fo	Con	Subtle variegation
Eranthus cicilica	**	B	10	Sh	Med	Fl	Wi	Yellow/Bronze foliage
E. hyemale	***	B	10	Sh	Med	Fl	Wi	Yellow
Eremurus bungei	***	B	130	S	Med	Fl	Su	Sharp yellow
E. robustus	***	B	240	S	Med	Fl	Su	Pink, huge!
Erodium chrysanthum	***	AH	10	S	Dry	Fl/Fo	Su	Lemon, ferny foliage
Erythronium species	***	B	20+	Sh	Med	Fl	Sp	Yellow, blue
Escallonia cultivars	*	W	180	S	Med	Fl	Su	Evergreen/flowers
Eschscholtzia californicum	***	A	30	S	Dry	Fl/Fo	Su	Orange shades
Euonymus europaeus 'Red Cascade'	***	W	240	S/Sh	Dry	Fr/Fo	Au	Pink fruit/Red foliage
Euphorbia amygdaloides, Woodspurge	***	H	60	Sh	Med	Fl/Fo	Sp	Green
– amygdaloides 'Rubra'	***	H	60	Sh	Med	Fl/Fo	Wi	Red/green foliage
E. characias and cultivars	***	H	75+	S	Dry	Fl	Wi/Sp	Lime green
E. palustris	**	H	75	S/Sh	Med	Fl	Sp/Su	Lime green
E. robbiae	***	H	GC 45	Sh	Dry	Fl/Fo	Con	Lime green
E. sikkimensis	*	H	75	Sh	Moist	Fo/Fl	Wi/Sp	Ruby shoots
Fagus sylvatica, Beech	***	W	3000+	S/Sh	Any	Fo	Con	Hedging, etc.
Filipendula ulmaria cultivars	**	H	75+	S/Sh	Moist	Fo/Fl	Sp/Su	Cream, golden
Forsythia viridissima 'Bronxensis'	*	W	45	S	Any	Fl	Wi	Yellow dwarf
Fremontodendron californicum	*	CW	500	S	Dry	Fl	Su	Sharp yellow
Fritillaria camschatcensis	**	B	45	Sh	Moist	Fl	Su	Black
F. imperialis, Crown Imperial	***	B	75	S	Med	Fl	Sp	Orange/yellow
F. meleagris, Snakes head	***	B	15	S	Med	Fl	Sp	Brown/white
F. persica	***	B	60	S	Dry	Fl	Sp	Dark brown

Plant name	LFG rate	Type	Hght/cms	Aspect	Conditions	Effect	Season	Colour
F. pyrenaica	*	B	15	S	Dry	Fl	Sp	Brown and yellow
Galanthus corcyrensis	***	B	10	S/Sh	Med	Fl	Au	White and green
G. elwesii	***	B	15	S/Sh	Med	Fl	Wi	White and green
G. nivalis + cultivars	***	B	10+	S/Sh	Med	Fl	Wi	White and green
G. n. subsp. reginae-olgae	***	B	10	S/Sh	Med	Fl	Au	White and green
G. n. 'Sam Arnott'	***	B	20	Sh	Med	Fl	Wi	Biggest snowdrop
Galtonia candicans	***	B	90	S	Any	Fl	Su	White
G. princeps	**	B	75	S	Med	Fl	Su	Green
Garrya elliptica	***	W	200	S/Sh	Any	Fo/Fl	Con	Catkins, evergreen
Genista 'Lydia'	*	W	45	S	Dry	Fl	Sp/Su	Yellow peaflowers
Gentiana acaulis	***	AH	15	S	Med	Fl	Sp	Deep blue
G. verna	**	AH	15	S	Med	Fl	Sp	Blue
Geranium farreri	***	AH	10	S	Dry	Fl	Sp/Su	Shell pink
G. pratense, Meadow cranesbill	***	H	75	S	Med	Fl	Su	Blue
Geum rivale cultivars	**	H	20	S/Sh	Med	Fl	Su	Pink/cream
Gladiolus byzantinus	**	B	60	S	Any	Fl	Su	Purple red
G. papilio	***	B	60	S	Med	Fl	Au	Purple and beige
Hacquetia epipactis	*	AH	15	Sh	Moist	Fl	Sp	Golden flowers
Hedera colchica	***	CW		Sh	Any	Fo	Con	Huge dark leaves
H. c. 'Paddy's Pride'	***	CW		Sh	Any	Fo	Con	Dark gold/green
H. helix cultivars, Ivy	***	CW	—	Sh	Any	Fo	Con	Diff. leaf forms
Helleborus corsicus	**	H	75	Sh	Any	Fo/Fl	Con	Green
H. foetidus, Stinking hellebore	**	H	60	Sh	Any	Fo/Fl	Con	Green
H. orientalis cultivars	***	H	60	Sh	Med	Fl	Wi/Sp	White/pink/damson
H. niger, Christmas rose	*	H	30	Sh/S	Med	Fl	Wi/Sp	White
Helianthemum nummularium cultivars	***	AH	15	S	Dry	Fl	Su	Red/pink/yellow
Helichrysum splendidum	*	W	90	S	Dry	Fo	Con	Tiny silver leaves
Hesperis matronalis, Dame's violet	**	H	75	S	Med	Fl	Su	Lilac mauve
Hosta all species	**	H	30+	Sh	Moist	Fo/Fl	Su	Leaf colour
Hoheria glabrata	*	W	200	S	Med°	Fl	Su	White
Hydrangea petiolaris	***	CW	360	Sh	Med	Fl/Fo	Su	Creamy white
Ilex aquifolium, Holly	***	W	1200+	S/Sh	Any	Fo/Fr	Con	Berries

Plant name	LFG rate	Type	Hght/cms	Aspect	Conditions	Effect	Season	Colour
Ilex a. 'Hascombensis'	* *	W	60	S/Sh	Any	Fo	Con	Dwarf holly
I. crenata	* *	W	45	S/Sh	Any	Fo	Con	Small evergreen
Inula hookeri	* *	H	60	S	Any	Fl	Su	Bright yellow
Ipheion uniflorum	* * *	B	15	S	Dry	Fl	Sp	Sky blue
I. magnifica	*	H	210	Sh	Moist	Fo/Fl	Su	Deep yellow
Iris chrysographes	*	H	60	S/Sh	Moist	Fl	Su	Purple-black
I. danfordiae	*	B	10	S	Dry	Fl	Wi	Yellow
Iris dwarf bearded hybrids	* * *	H	20	S	Dry	Fl	Sp	All colours
I. pseudacorus	* * *	H	60	S	Wet	Fl	Su	Yellow
I. sibirica	* *	H	90	Sh	Moist	Fl/Fo	Su	Blues to white
Juniperus communis 'Compressa'	*	W	30	S	Dry	Fo	Con	Dwarf juniper
J. conferta	*	W	30	S/Sh	Any	Fo	Con	Evergreen
Knautia arvensis, Field scabious	* *	H	60	S	Dry	Fl	Su	Blue
Kniphofia hybrids, Pokers	* *	H	45+	S	Dry	Fl	Su/Au	Cream/orange
Lamium album	*	H	45	S	Any	Fl	Sp/Su	White invasive
L. maculatum	* * *	H	30	S/Sh	Any	Fl/Fo	Con	Pink/white
L. m. 'White Nancy'	* * *	H	20	Sh	Any	Fo/Fl	Con	Silver/white
Lapageria rosea	*	CW	300+	Sh	Med°	Fl	Su/Au	Pink, evergreen
Lathyrus latifolius	* * *	CH	120	S	Any	Fl	Su	Pink/white
L. laxiflorus	* * *	H	20	S	Any	Fl	Su	Blue and white
L. rotundifolius	* * *	CH	100	S	Any	Fl	Su	Brick pink
Lavandula spica, Lavender	* * *	W	30+	S	Dry	Fl/Fo	Con	Blue/lavender/white
Lavandula stoechas	*	W(T)	45	S	Dry	Fl/Fo	Con	Blue aromatic
Leucojum vernum	* *	B	20	S	Moist	Fl	Wi	White and green
L. aestivum	* *	B	30	Sh	Any	Fl	Sp	White and green
Ligularia clivorum cultivars	* * *	H	120+	S/Sh	Moist	Fl/Fo	Su	Orange/yellow
Lilium auratum and hybrids	*	B	90+	S/Sh	Med°	Fl	Su/Au	All shades
L. martagon	* * *	B	90	Sh	Med	Fl	Su	Purple/white
L. henryi	* * *	B	180	S/Sh	Med	Fl	Su	Pale orange
L. pardalinum	*	B	60	Sh	Moist°	Fl	Su	Orange and yellow
L. speciosum and hybrids	*	B	90+	S/Sh	Med°	Fl	Su/Au	All shades/scent
L. tigrinum	* * *	B	100	S	Med	Fl	Su	Orange
Limnanthes douglasii	* * *	A	15	S	Any	Fl/Fo	Sp/Su	Yellow and white
Lobelia cardinalis 'Queen Victoria'	* *	P	60	S	Moist	Fl/Fo	Su/Au	Red/purple foliage
Lonicera fragrantissima	* *	W	240	S	Med	Fl	Wi	White, fragrant
L. japonica Halliana	* * *	CW	GC	Sh	Any	Fl	Su	Evergreen, scent

Plant name	LFG rate	Type	Hght/cms	Aspect	Conditions	Effect	Season	Colour
L. periclymenum, Honeysuckle	*	CW		Sh	Any	Fl	Su	Yellow, scent
L. p. 'Belgica'	***	CW		S/Sh	Med	Fl	Sp/Su	Early, red/yellow
Lunaria biennis, Honesty	***	A	75	S/Sh	Med	Fl	Sp	Magenta/white
L. rediviva, Perennial Honesty	***	H	60	Sh	Med	Fl	Sp	Lilac
Lupinus polyphyllus	***	H	75	S	Med	Fl	Sp/Su	Blue/pink shades
Lychnis coronaria	**	H	60	S	Any	Fl/Fo	Su	Wine/silver foliage
Mahonia japonica	**	W	100	Sh	Med	Fl	Wi	Primrose/scent
Magnolia grandiflora	**	W	750+	S	Any°	Fo/Fl	Con	Big cream flowers
M. 'Undulata'	***	W	120	Sh	Any	Fo	Con	Lustrous green foliage
Malva moschata, Musk Mallow	***	H	75	S	Any	Fl	Su	Pink
M. m. 'Alba'	***	H	60	S	Any	Fl	Su	Excellent white
Maurandia erubescens	*	CH(T)	180+	S	Med	Fl	Su	Pink trumpets
Meconopsis betonicifolia	*	H	60	Sh	Moist	Fl	Su	Blue
M. cambrica, Welsh poppy	*	H	30	Sh	Any	Fl	Su	Yellow
Mentha aquatica, Water mint	**	H	45	S	Wet	Fo	Su	Aromatic
M. spicata and varieties	*	H	45+	S	Any	Fo	Su	Mints invasive
Mimulus guttatus	**	H	45	S	Wet	Fl	Su	Yellow
Myosotis alpestris, Forgetmenot	**	A	15	S	Any	Fl	Sp	Blue
M. scorpioides, Water F.	***	H	30	S	Wet	Fl	Su	Bright blue
Myrrhis odorata, Sweet cicely	*	H	60	Sh	Any	Fl/Fo	Sp/Su	White, aromatic
Narcissus bulbocodium	***	B	15	S	Moist	Fl	Sp	Yellow/citron
N. cyclamineus and cultivars	***	B	15	S	Moist	Fl	Sp	Yellow
N. jonquilla	**	B	20	S	Med	Fl	Sp	Yellow/scent
N. juncifolius	**	B	20	S	Med	Fl	Sp	Buttercup yellow
N. poeticus 'recurvus'	***	B	30	S	Med	Fl	Sp	White/scent
N. pseudonarcissus and cultivars	***	B	20+	S/Sh	Med	Fl	Sp	Yellow
Nemophila insignis	*	A	30	Sh	Moist	Fl	Su	Blue
Oenothera tetragona cultivars	**	H	30	S	Dry	Fl	Su	Yellow
Omphalodes verna	*	H	15	Sh	Med	Fl/Fo	Sp	Blue
Origanum laevigatum	*	H	30	S	Dry	Fl	Su	Purple
Osteospermum ecklonis	**	H(T)	30	S	Dry	Fl	Su	Whitish blue
O. jucundum hybrids	**	H(T)	30	S	Dry	Fl	Su	Cream/mauve/purple
Paeonia obovata 'Alba'	**	H	60	S/Sh	Med	Fl/Fo	Sp/Su	Bronze foliage
P. Chinese cultivars	***	H	60+	S	Med	Fl	Su	Pink/white shades
P. officinalis cultivars	*	H	60	S	Med	Fl	Sp	Red/pink/white
P. suffruticosa cultivars	*	W	75+	S	Med	Fl	Su	Red/pink/white
Papaver orientale hybrids	*	H	100	S	Med	Fl	Su	Red/maroon/white
P. rhoeas, Field poppy	*	A	30	S	Any	Fl	Su	Red

Plant name	LFG rate	Type	Hght/cms	Aspect	Conditions	Effect	Season	Colour
P. rhoeas, 'Shirley poppies'	**	A	30	S	Any	Fl	Su	Red/Pink/White
P. somniferum	**	A	75	S	Any	Fl/Fo	Su	Mixed/invasive
Parthenocissus henryana	**	CW		S/Sh	Med	Fo	Su	Purple foliage
Penstemon campanulatus hybrids	***	H	45+	S	Med	Fl	Su	Pink, small flowers
P. gloxinioides hybrids	*	H(T)	45+	S	Med	Fl	Su	Blue/purple shades
P. hartwegii hybrids	***	H	45+	S	Med	Fl	Su	Red shades
Philadelphus coronaria 'Aurea'	**	W	150	Sh	Med	Fo	Su	Gold leaves
P. 'Manteau d'Hermine'	*	W	100	S/Sh	Any	Fl	Su	Dwarf mock orange
Physocarpus opulifolius 'Dart's Gold'	*	W	100	Sh	Med	Fo	Sp/Su	Gold foliage
Piptanthus laburnifolius	*	W(T)	180	S	Med	Fl/Fo	Su	Yellow peaflowers
Polemonium foliosissimum cultivars	*	H	30+	S	Med	Fl	Su	Blue/mauve/white
Polygonatum multiflorum, Solomon's Seal	***	H	90	Sh	Med	Fl/Fo	Sp	White bells
Polygonum affine	**	H	GC	S/Sh	Med	Fo/Fl	Su/Au	Pink/red
Potentilla atrosanguinea	*	H	45	S	Med	Fl/Fo	Su	Blood red
P. nepalensis cultivars	**	H	45	S	Med	Fl	Su	Pink
P. recta 'Sulphurea'	*	H	60	S	Med	Fl	Su	Lemon
P. rupestris	*	H	30	S	Med	Fl	Sp	White
Primula elatior, Oxlip	***	H	30	Sh	Med	Fl	Sp	Butter yellow
P. 'Candelabra' hybrids and specs	**	H	60+	Sh	Moist	Fl	Su	Orange/red/yellow
P. florindae	***	H	60	Sh	Moist	Fl	Su	Mid yellow
P. veris, Cowslip	***	H	20	S	Any	Fl	Sp	Yellow wildflower
P. vulgaris, Primrose	***	H	15	Sh	Moist	Fl	Sp	Pale yellow
P. vulgaris hybrids (old)	***	H	15	Sh	Moist	Fl	Sp	Pink/mauve/etc.
Prunella grandiflora cultivars	***	H	20	S	Med	Fl	Su	Pink/mauve/white
Prunus most species eg:								
P. avium, Wild Cherry, Gean	**	W	1500+	S/Sh	Any	Fl	Sp	White blossom
P. laurocerasus 'Marbled White'	*	W	150	Sh	Any	Fo	Con	Variegated laurel
P. prostata	*	W	30	S	Dry	Fl	Sp	Pink
P. sargentii	***	W	1000+	S/Sh	Med	Fo/Fl	Sp/Au	Pink flowers/red foliage
P. 'Tai Haku'	***	H	1200	S	Any	Fl/Fo	Sp	White blossom
P. tenella 'Fire Hill'	*	W	90	S	Any	Fl	Sp	Pink dwarf almond

Plant name	LFG rate	Type	Hght/cms	Aspect	Conditions	Effect	Season	Colour
P. 'Umineko'	**	H	300	S	Any	Fl/Fo	Sp/Au	White flowers/yellow foliage
Pulmonaria angustifolia	***	H	30	Sh	Moist	Fl/Fo	Sp	Dark blue
P. rubra cultivars	*	H	35	Sh	Med	Fl	Sp	Pink only/no spots
P. saccharata cultivars	***	H	30	Sh	Moist	Fl/Fo	Con	Pink, blue and spots
Pulsatilla vulgaris and cultivars	***	H	20	S	Dry	Fl	Sp	Blue/white/wine
Pyracantha cultivars	**	W	200+	S	Any	Fr	Au	Berries
Ranunculus acris, Meadow buttercup	*	H	60	S	Any	Fl	Sp/Su	Invasive
R. ficaria and cultivars, Celandine	*	H	10	S/Sh	Any	Fl	Sp	Shiny yellow
Rhamnus cathartica, Buckthorn	*	W	350	S/Sh	Any	Fo/Fr	Au	Black berries
R. frangula, Alder buckthorn	*	W	240	S/Sh	Any	Fr	Au	Pink berries
Rheum palmatum 'Atrosanguineum'	**	W	180	S/Sh	Moist	Fo/Fl	Su	Huge foliage
Rhododendron calostrotum 'Gigha'	*	W	60	Sh	Med°	Fl/Fo	Sp	Red
R. ferrugineum, Alpenrose	*	W	45	Su	Moist	Fl	Su	Pink
R. scintillans	*	W	60	Sh	Med°	Fl	Sp	Blue
R. yakushimanum hybrids	*	W	60	S/Sh	Med°	Fl/Fo	Sp/Su	Pink/cream
Ribes sanguineum, Flowering currant	*	W	240	S	Any	Fl	Sp	Red blossoms
Rodgersia all species	**	H	90+	Sh	Moist	Fo	Su	Foliage
Robinia hispida	*	W	600	S	Dry	Fl/Fo	Su	Pink peaflowers
R. pseudoacacia 'Frisia'	**	W	600	S	Dry	Fo	Su	Golden foliage
Romneya coulteri	***	H	120	S	Dry	Fl	Su	White and yellow
Rosa: see separate list, p. 138								
Rubus lineatus	***	W(T)	120	S	Med	Fo	Su	Palmate foliage
R. odoratus	***	W	150	Sh	Moist	Fo/Fl	Su	Magenta
R. × tridel 'Benenden'	***	W	400	S	Any	Fl/Fo	Sp	Huge, white flowers
R. spectabilis	***	W	120	Sh	Moist	Fl	Sp	Rich pink
Salix fargesii	***	W	180	S/Sh	Moist	Fo/St	Con	Red twigs
S. grahami	***	W	10	Sh	Dry	Fo/St	Wi/Su	Shrubby dwarf
S. helvetica	***	W	60	S/Sh	Med	Fo/St	Con	Silver foliage
S. hylamatica	***	AH	10	Sh	Any	St/Fl	Con	Red catkins
S. lanata	***	W	60	S	Any	Fo/St	Con	Silver foliage

Plant name	LFG rate	Type	Hght/cms	Aspect	Conditions	Effect	Season	Colour
Salix melanostachys	**	W	120	S/Sh	Med	Fl/St	Con	Black catkins
Salvia horminum	***	A	30	S	Dry	Fl	Su/Au	Pink, blue, white
S. officinalis, Sage	***	H	45	S	Dry	Fo/Fl	Con	Blue flowers/aromatic
S. patens	*	T	45	S	Dry	Fl	Su/Au	Deep blue
S. rutilans	*	T	90	S	Dry	Fo/Fl	Su	Red/aromatic
Sanguisorba minor, Salad burnet	**	H	20	S	Dry	Fo/Fl	Sp/Su	Meadow plant
S. officinalis, Burnet	**	H	90	S	Med	Fl	Su	Maroon flowers
Saponaria ocymoides	**	AH	15	S	Any	Fl	Su	Pink
Saxifraga granulata	***	H	20	S	Med	Fl	Su	White
S. × Urbium, London Pride	***	AH	20	S/Sh	Any	Fl/Fo	Con	Pink flowers
Schizostylis coccinea and cultivars	***	B	30	S	Dry	Fl	Au/Wi	Pink shades
Scilla non-scripta, Bluebell	***	B	30	Sh	Moist	Fl	Sp	Blue/scent
S. sibirica	***	B	15	S	Med	Fl	Sp	Bright blue
Silene alba, White campion	**	H	60	S	Any	Fl	Su	Invasive
S. dioica, Red Campion	**	H	60	Sh	Any	Fl	Sp/Su	Pink
Sisyrinchium bermudianum	**	H	20	S	Any	Fl	Su	Blue
S. biscutellum	**	H	20	S	Any	Fl	Su	Buff
S. striatum	***	H	60	S	Med	Fl	Su	Pale straw
Smilacina racemosa	**	H	60	Sh	Med	Fl	Sp	Creamy plumes
S. stellata	*	H	45	Sh	Med	Fl/Fo	Sp	Tiny white stars
Solanum crispum	*	CW(T)	500	S	Med	Fl	Su	Blue
S. c. 'Glasnevin'	**	CW	500	S	Med	Fl	Su/Au	Blue, vigorous
Sorbus species esp:								
S. aria 'Lutescens'	**	W	900	S/Sh	Any	Fo	Con	Silver foliage
S. aucuparia cultivars, Rowans	***	W	600+	S/Sh	Any	Fo/Fr	Con	All desirable
S. cashmiriana	***	W	900	S/Sh	Med	Fl/Fr	Con	Pink flowers/white fruit
Sternbergia lutea	*	B	10	S	Dry	Fl	Au	Yellow
Stranvaesia davidiana	*	W	180	S/Sh	Med	Fr/Fo	Au	Red berries
Symphoriocarpus rivularis	*	W	180	S/Sh	Any	Fr	Au/Wi	White berries
Symphytum grandiflorum cultivars	***	H	30+	S/Sh	Any	Fo/Fl	Sp/Su	White/blue/pink
S. × uplandicum 'Variegatum'	**	H	75	Sh	Moist	Fl	Su	Cream edged
Syringa josiflexa	**	W	300+	S	Any	Fl	Sp	Pale pink
S. vulgaris 'Madame lemoine'	*	W	300	S	Any	Fl	Sp	Double white

Plant name	LFG rate	Type	Hght/cms	Aspect	Conditions	Effect	Season	Colour
S. v. 'Firmament'	*	W	300	S	Any	Fl	Sp	Lilac-blue
Taxus baccata, Yew	**	W	1800+	S/Sh	Any	Fo	Con	Hedging, etc.
Tellima grandiflora 'Rubra'	*	H	GC 45	Sh	Any	Fo	Con	Creamy flowers
Thymus citriodorus	***	W	20	S	Dry	Fl/Fo	Con	Mauve, aromatic
T. × 'Doone Valley'	***	W	15	S	Dry	Fo	Con	Gold variegated
T. vulgaris cultivars, Wild Thyme	***	AH	10	S	Dry	Fl/Fo	Sp/Su	Purple/pink/white
Tropaeolum canariense	**	CH	200	S	Med	Fl	Su	Yellow
T. speciosum	***	CH	240+	Sh	Med	Fl	Su	Scarlet
T. hybrids (nasturtiums)	***	A	—	S	Dry	Fl	Su	Orange/yellow
Trillium grandiflorum	**	H	30	Sh	Med°	Fl	Sp	White
Tulbaghia violacea	***	B(T)	45	S	Dry	Fl	Su/Au	Lilac mauve
Tulipa clusiana	*	B	20	S	Med	Fl	Sp	Pink and white
T. fosteriana cultivars	***	B	60	S	Med	Fl	Sp	Red/creamy white
T. sprengeri	***	B	45	S/Sh	Med	Fl	Sp/Su	Scarlet
T. turkestanica	**	B	30	S	Dry	Fl	Sp	Cream/yellow
T. whitallii	***	B	30	S	Dry	Fl	Sp	Bright orange
Veronica gentianoides	*	H	30	S	Med	Fl	Su	Pale blue
V. rupestris	**	AH	15	S	Dry	Fl	Su	Blue/pink
Verbascum blattaria 'alba'	**	H	100	S	Dry	Fl	Su	Beige to white
Verbena bonariense	***	H(T)	120	S	Any	Fl	Su	Purple
V. bombyciferum	*	H	240	S	Dry	Fo/Fl	Su	Yellow/Silver leaf
Viburnum lantana, Wayfaring tree	*	W	180	S/Sh	Any	Fl/Fr	Su	White flowers/Red berry
V. odoratissimum	**	W	180	S	Med	Fo	Su	Glossy leaves
V. opulus, Guelder rose	*	W	200	S/Sh	Dry	Fl/Fr	Su	White flowers/Red berry
V. rhytidophyllum	**	W	300	S/Sh	Any	Fo	Con	Bold foliage
Vinca major and V. minor cultivars	***	W	GC	Sh	Any	Fl/Fo	Con	Blue/purple/white
Viola cornuta cultivars	***	H	20	S/Sh	Any	Fl	Con	Blue/white/lilac
V. cucculata – see V. papilionacea								
V. elatior	*	H	45	Sh	Med	Fl	Su	Pale blue
V. odorata cultivars	**	H	15	Sh	Moist	Fl	Wi/Sp	Blue/white/pink
V. papilonacea forms	**	H	15	Sh	Med	Fl	Sp	Blue/white shades
V. riviniana cultivars	*	H	10	Sh/S	Any	Fl	Sp	Blue/pink/white
V. tricolor hybrids	**	H	15	S	Any	Fl	Con	All shades

Plant name	LFG rate	Type	Hght/cms	Aspect	Conditions	Effect	Season	Colour
Wisteria japonica cultivars	*	CW	—	S	Dry	Fl	Sp	Blue/pink/white
Wisteria sinensis	***	CW	—	S	Dry	Fl	Sp	Blue
Xeranthemum annuum	**	A	30	S	Dry	Fl	Su	Pink/white
Yucca filamentosa	*	W	90	S	Dry	Fl	Su	Cream

Selected *laissez-faire* roses

Rosa   Roses enjoy medium to heavy, fertile soil in full light.

Plant name	LFG rate	Type	Hght/cms	Colour
Adam messerich	**	W	180	Rich pink, fragrant, recurrent
Agnes	***	W	150	Soft yellow, recurrent, scented rugosa
Alba maxima	*	W	150	White, scented, non-recurrent
Alberic Barbier	***	CW	400	Lemon white rambler, recurrent
Arthur Hillier	***	W	240	Single, deep pink, hips
Blanc Double de Coubert	***	W	150	Scented, white double rugosa
Bobbie James	**	CW	700	Cream rambler, rampant
Buff Beauty	***	W	180	Apricot, recurrent, scented
Canary bird	*	W	240	Sharp yellow single, non-recurrent
Cecile Brunner	***	W	90	Shell pink, tiny buds, recurrent
Charles de Mills	***	W	130	Dark red, scented, non-recurrent
Claire Rose	*	W	120	Pale pink, recurrent English rose
Conrad F. Meyer	**	W	200	Pale pink, fragrant, recurrent
Cornelia	***	W	150	Dark pink buds open salmon, recurrent
Fantin Latour	***	W	150	Pale blush pink, scent, non-recurrent
Felicia	***	W	150	Salmon, recurrent, scent
Félicité Parmentier	***	W	120	Pale blush, scent, non-recurrent

Plant name	LFG rate	Type	Hght/cms	Colour
Frau Dagmar Hastrup	***	W	120	Pale pink single rugosa, fruits
Fritz Nobis	*	W	160	Pink shrub, non-recurrent
Frühlingsgold	***	W	240	Vigorous, yellow, non-recurrent
Frühlingsmorgen	**	W	210	Single pink and cream, non-recurrent
Gloire de Dijon	**	CW	300	Beige, recurrent, scented
Goldfinch	***	CW	300	Apricot cream, non-recurrent
Graham Thomas	*	W	120	Strong yellow recurrent English rose
Hermosa	***	W	120	Pale pink, recurrent, scent
Iceberg	*	W	120	White repeater, no scent
Ispahan	**	W	180	Pink, non-recurrent, scent
Lady Hillingdon	***	CW	300	Large apricot, fragrant
Kathleen Harrop	*	CW	180	Pale pink, recurrent, scent
Lordly Oberon	*	W	120	Pink, recurrent English rose
Maiden's Blush	**	W	140	Blush pink, scented, non-recurrent
Marguerite Hilling	**	W	160	Pink, slightly recurrent shrub
Mary Rose	*	W	120	Pale pink, recurrent English rose
Max Graf	**	W	GC	Pink flower, ground cover rose
Mermaid	*	CW	360	Single yellow, recurrent
Mme Gregoire Staechelin	See Spanish Beauty			
Mrs Anthony Waterer	***	W	150	Wine red, recurrent, scented rugosa
Nevada	***	W	180	Cream shrub, slightly recurrent
Nozomi	*	W	GC	Single flowered, white ground cover
Old Pink Moss	**	W	120	Sweet scented moss rose
Paul's Himalayan Musk	*	CW	500	Small, white flowered rampant rambler
Paul's Lemon Pillar	**	CW	300	Large, lemon white, fragrant
Pax	**	W	150	White, fragrant, recurrent
Prosperity	***	W	150	Lemon white, fragrant, recurrent
Penelope	***	W	150	Salmon, recurrent, scented
Perle d'Or	***	W	90	Tiny salmon buds, recurrent
Raubritter	*	W	GC	Low mound of double pink flowers
R. andersonii	**	W	150	Single pink, non-recurrent, hips
R. banksiae lutea	*	CW	500	Yellow clusters – warm wall
R. californica semi-plena	*	W	210	Semi double pink flowers, non-recurrent
R. eglanteria hybrids	*	W	180	Scented foliage

Plant name	LFG rate	Type	Hght/cms	Colour
R. filipes	*	CW	900	Rampant, white rambler
R. helenae	*	CW	360	Clusters of little hips
R. holodonta	*	W	180	Elongated hips
R. × highdownensis	*	W	240	Huge shrub, fragrant pink flowers
Rosa Mundi	***	W	100	Striped pink/lilac, scented
R. moyesii	***	W	200	Red, single, non-recurrent, Hips
R. roxburghii	*	W	180	Pink flowers, odd prickly hips
R. sericea 'Pteracantha'	*	W	180	Red, translucent thorns
R. spinossissima, Burnet rose	**	W	90	Suckering, White, scented flowers
R. s. 'Dunwich'	**	W	90	Suckering, cream single flowers
R. villosa	*	W	180	Pink non-recurrent, hairy red hips
Rosaraie de l'Haÿ	***	W	180	Purple-crimson, recurrent, scented
Sarah van Fleet	***	W	150	Pale pink, scented, recurrent rugosa
Scarlet Fire	**	W	180	Scarlet, single, good hips, scentless
Snow Carpet	*	W	GC	White, small ground-cover rose
Spanish Beauty	**	CW	300	Blowsy pink, non-recurrent
Stanwell Perpetual	***	W	150	White flush pink, recurrent, scent
The Squire	*	W	120	Crimson, recurrent English rose
Tuscany Superb	*	W	100	Claret petals, gold sepals, scent
Veilchenblau	**	CW	300	Liverish purple, non-recurrent
Vick's Caprice	**	W	120	Deep pink striped lilac, recurrent
Wedding Day	*	CW	700	Single, apricot cream, rambler
William III	***	W	90	Suckering, scented pink burnet
William Lobb	*	W	180	Wine red moss rose, non-recurrent
Zephirine Drouhin	***	CW	240	Purple pink, recurrent, scent

INDEX

Note: See also plant list, pp. 124–140 for plants not mentioned elsewhere in the text.

Index

Index